ANTARCTICA
AN INTRODUCTORY GUIDE

Diana Galimberti

ANTARCTICA
AN INTRODUCTORY GUIDE

ZAGIER & URRUTY
PUBLICATIONS

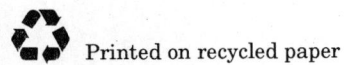 Printed on recycled paper

ZAGIER & URRUTY
PUBLICATIONS

6630 Indian creek Dr. # 223 - Miami Beach, FL 33141-5840 - (305) 865-5002

PUBLISHERS OF:

Libros de Viaje Sol
Tierra del Fuego Magazine
The First Adventure Handbook of Southern South America

Distributed in Europe by:
Altaïr - Balmes 69 - E 08007 Barcelona - Spain
Phone (34-3) 254-2966 - FAX (34-3) 451-2559

Purchases from other countries:
Zagier & Urruty - P.O. Box 94 Suc. 19 - 1419 Buenos Aires - Argentina
Phone (54-1) 572-1050 - FAX (54-1) 572-5766

To the polar ship "A.R.A. BAHIA PARAISO",
for what it has meant to me
in my discovery of Antarctica,
and for what it has taught all of us
about the special care
the white continent deserves.

Contents

Invertebrates - Finfish - Marine mammals - Pinnipeds (seals) - Antarctic fur seal - Crabeater seal - Weddell seal - Ross seal - Leopard seal - Elephant seal - Cetaceans (whales) - Blue whale - Fin whale - Sei whale - Minke whale - Humpback whale - Southern Right whale - Sperm whale - Killer whale - Birds - Penguins - Adelies, Gentoos and Chinstraps - Emperors - Kings - Macaronis and Rockhoppers - Seabirds - Albatross - Petrels and fulmars - Cormorant - Skua - Snowy sheatbill - Southern gull - Antarctic tern.

Premise - Historical stages - Magellan (1520) - Hoces and Drake (1526 and 1578) - Schouten and Le Maire (1616) - 1700s - Cook (1770-75) - 1800s - Sealers - Smith (1818) - Palmer - Powell - Bellinghausen (1819-21) - Weddell (1820-24) - Foster (1828-29) - Biscoe (1830-32) - Early scientific voyages - D'Urville (1837-40) - Wilkes (1838-41) - Ross (1839-43) - Steam navigation era - Whalers - 1st International Polar Year (1882-83) - 6th International Congress of Geography (1895) - Gerlache - Borchgrevink - 7th International Congress of Geography (1899) - Drygalsky (1901-04) - Nordenskjöld (1901-04) - Scott (1901-04) - Bruce (1902-04) - Charcot (1903-05 and 1908-10) - The heroic era - Shackleton (1907-09) - Amundsen and Scott (1911-12) - Shackleton (1914-15) - Aeroplane era - Expansion phase - International Geophysical Year (1957-58) - Antarctic Treaty (1959).

International context - Antarctic Treaty - Content of the Treaty - Peaceful purposes - Freedom of science - Right to inspection - Freezing of sovereign rights - Claimed sectors - Offshore jurisdiction - Consultative Meetings - Status of the Parties - Criticisms of Treaty selectivity - Revision mechanism - Recommendations - Seal Convention (CCAS) - Convention on Marine Living Resources (CCAMLR) - Mineral Convention (CRAMRA).

International Geophysical Year (1957-58) - Scientific Committee on Antarctic Research (SCAR) - Working groups - SCAR functions - International organizations - Conservation organizations - Antarctic stations - Early permanent stations - Station distribution

- Station category - Station structure and logistics - Antarctic population - Research fields - Atmospheric sciences - Glaciology - Earth sciences - Oceanography - Biology and environmental studies .

Historical background - International background - Sealing - Whaling - Hunting pattern - Annual catch - Whaling consequences - International Whaling Commission - Marine living resources - Finfish exploitation - Impact of fishery - Krill exploitation - Harvesting volumes - Present stocks - Krill surplus - Mineral exploitation - Hypothetical resource - Prospecting methods - Metals - Coal - Hydrocarbons - Sedimetary basins - Exploitation requirements - Ice exploitation - Tourism - Regulation of tourism.

Ecosystem fragility - Ecosystem organization - World relevance - Local impacts - Station impact - Adopted measures - Waste disposal - Logistical risks - Energy production - External impacts - Contamination - Greenhouse effect - Consequences - Ozone question - Ozone generation and destruction - Possible causes - CFC hypothesis - Consequences - Preventive measures.

Extracts from recommendations and measures adopted by the Antarctic Treaty Consultative States about tourism and the behavior of visitors to Antarctica.

List of the Antarctic National Committees of the SCAR member States.

Visiting Antarctica: some practical suggestions.

Preface

My professional experience of several visits to Antarctica and of life in Tierra del Fuego has led me, after a number of years, to pause to consider my everyday involvement in general environmental concerns, with particular regard to tourism in these unusual sites of special natural interest.

In recent years, the issue of tourism in Antarctica has become an important subject of international debate because of the negative impact it may have on the local environment if allowed to develop without adequate control or discrimination. Until now, the international community has not adopted a definitive policy for tourism and is at present in a transition phase, characterized by the need to understand whether, when, where and how tourism may be managed in Antarctica.

From my childhood I had always dreamt of visiting Antarctica and, though I can now look at it through professional eyes, I never wish to forget the spirit of mystery mixed with curiosity, wonder and respect which stimulated me so many years ago. I have never thought of myself as a tourist in Antarctica, but simply as a *visitor* to an unknown land, rather like past explorers who experienced the most remarkable adventures in the world's most extraordinary environment.

Years and dreams have passed, but the desire to share the excitement of preparing a real or imaginary journey to Antarctica with anyone similarly fascinated by the white continent, has led me to write this introductory guide. With it, I hope to give a general view of Antarctica's geological, biological, political and economic features, which I consider to be a base for a broader understanding of its dynamics and the uniqueness of its environment. This approach may perhaps be helpful in seeing the subject of tourism in Antarctica in a more comprehensive context and in understanding better why it has become such a controversial issue. Hopefully, this may also allow us to consider the question not simply as a theoretical object of international concern, but as an area in which each of us has a role to play.

I am not inclined to judge whether tourism in Antarctica is *per se* good or bad; the important question seems to me to be rather *how* tourism in Antarctica is managed. I personally hold the optimistic belief that man has the capacity to choose his relationship with the environment in which he lives, and to establish a mechanism to control the impact of his activities on nature. If this is true, then a responsible and effective policy may be adopted to allow us to enjoy and make use of an environment as unique even as Antarctica, without necessarily disrupting its ecological balance. Conversely, the necessity of banning general access to the white continent would be for me a sad demonstration of man's incompatibility with nature and a major defeat in broad cultural terms.

Although the issue of tourism involves political and economic interests at a high international level, the individual wishing to travel to Antarctica may also make a personal contribution to the view that man is able to coexist with nature and that his presence on the continent is not necessarily destructive. He can do this by considering himself a responsible visitor rather than a passive tourist, with exactly the same consciousness and respect for the local environment as all Antarctic inhabitants. This implies an awareness of the right to enjoy and make use of a trip to Antarctica as a rewarding and instructive experience, while remembering our duty to preserve the continent for future generations.

D. G.

Introduction

In recent years Antarctica has become a fundamental issue in the debate on the management of world affairs because of its far-reaching political, economic, cultural and environmental implications. In spite of the many different views on its present and future administration there is, however, unanimous agreement that Antarctica is not simply one more region of the globe to be preserved, but an extraordinary continent which deserves very special attention. The white continent is not only an absolutely unique ecosystem, but is also a fundamental key to the understanding of world phenomena such as adaptation dynamics and geophysical processes, as well as an important touchstone for present world trends in the environmental field.

The significance of Antarctica as a "well of knowledge" has been ensured until now by its virtually untouched environment, undoubtedly the least altered by man's activities, preserved through the centuries by its geographical isolation and its physical inaccessibility. The question today is whether the technological progress of the industrial age, which has provided on the one hand the logistical means to gain access to the continent, and on the other the scientific know-how to study it, will be able to preserve Antarctica as the "last untouched land" on earth.

The aim of this introductory guide is to provide a comprehensive view of the past, present and future of Antarctica, as far as its geography, geological evolution, biology, history, environment and legal and economic aspects are concerned. It is intended to offer to anyone wishing to acquire a basic knowledge of Antarctica, without needing a scientific or technical background, the foundation for a better understanding of the reality behind its evocative name, and a consideration of the reasons why it has become the object of so much interest on a world scale.

A better comprehension of Antarctica may eventually contribute to a feeling of personal involvement in the environmental issues it raises, and thus to an appreciation that the preservation of the continent is not simply a theoretical or abstract question, but a reality in which everyone has a part.

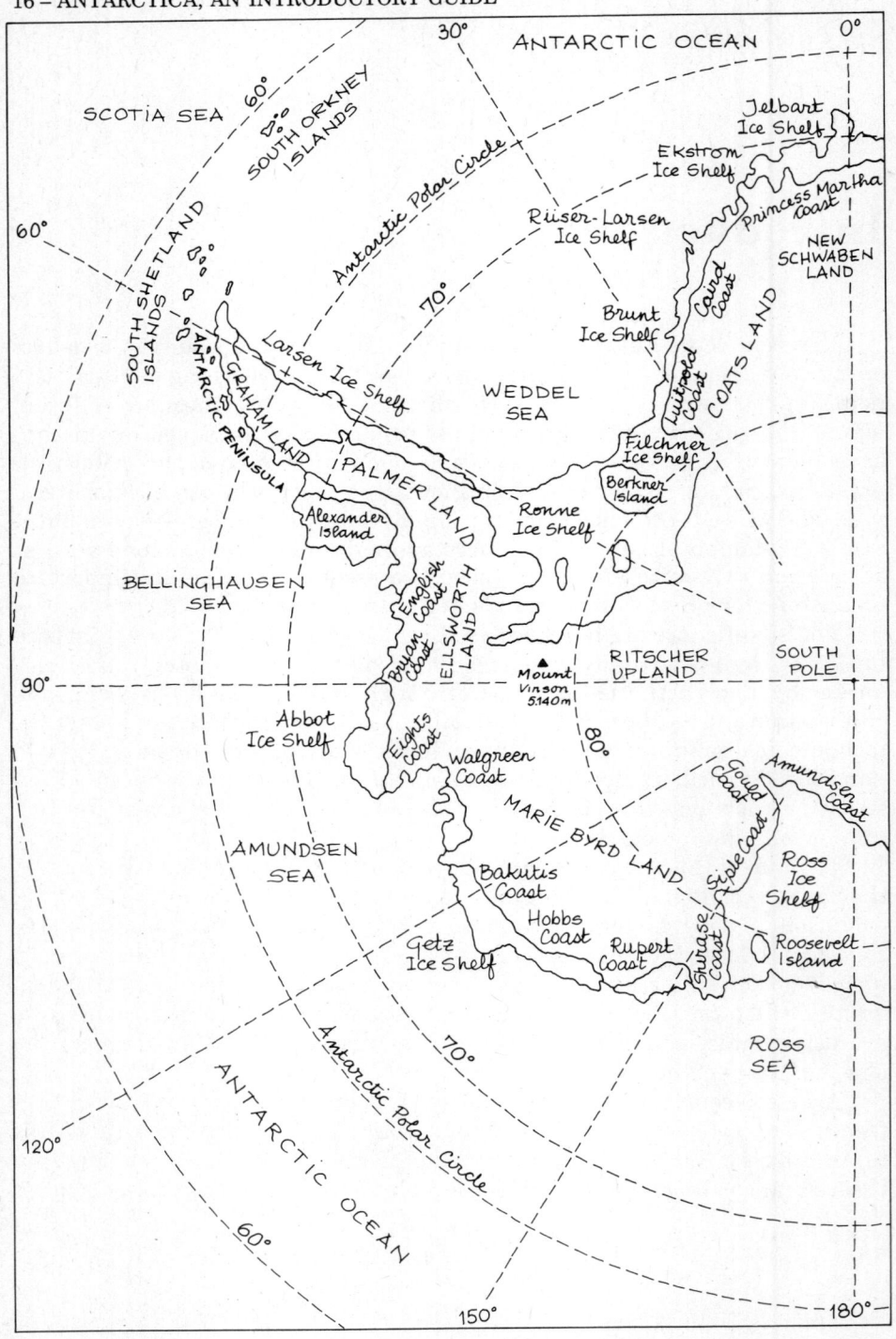

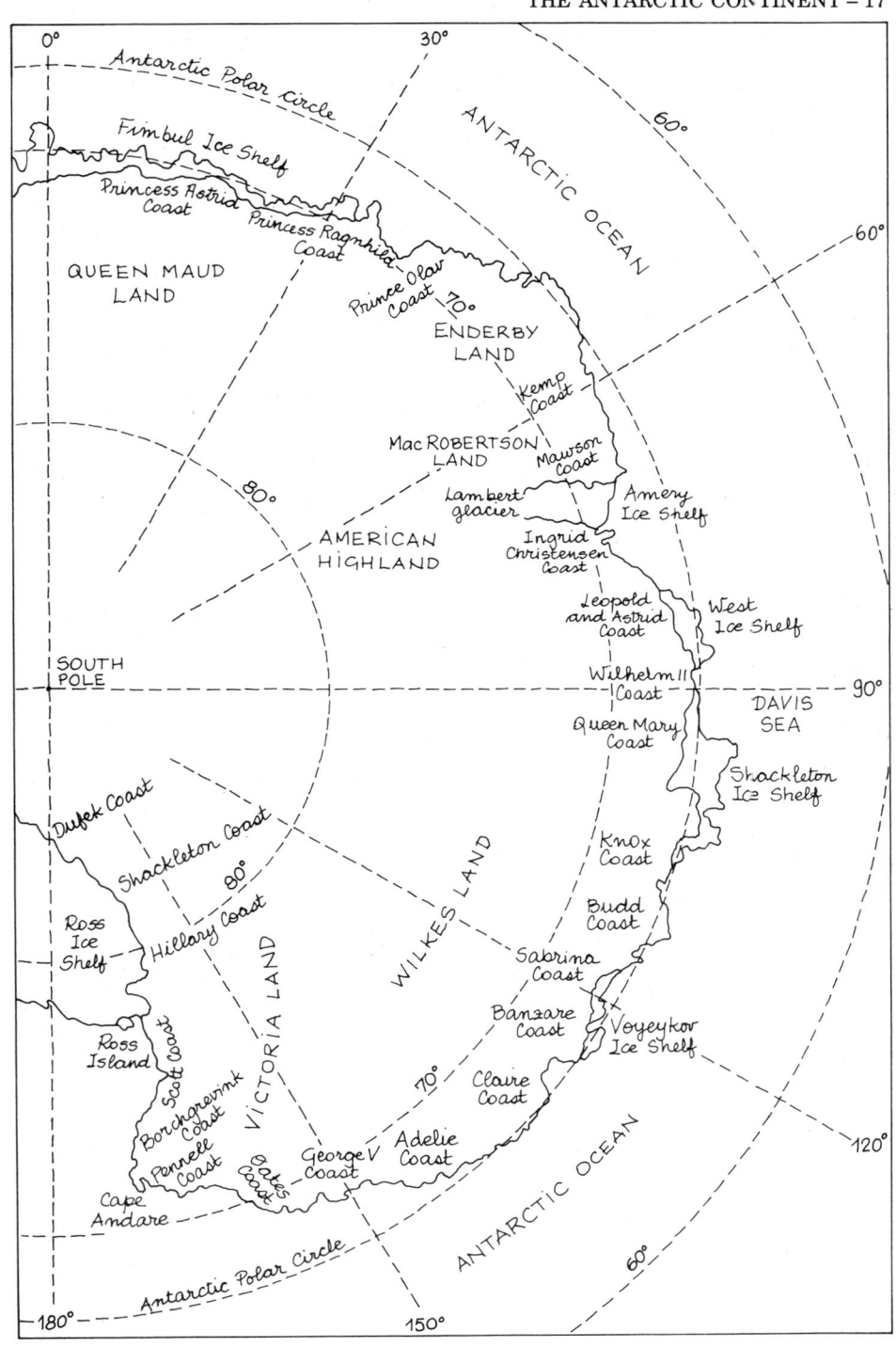

CHAPTER 1

Geographical introduction

The extreme continent

Antarctica is a geographical unit distinguished by the most extraordinary features existing on earth, the best definition of which is *extreme*. In effect its extreme circumpolar position governs its environmental dynamics, which are different even from those of its symmetric opposite, the Arctic, an ocean permanently covered by floating marine ice.

Antarctica, in contrast, is a continent almost completely submerged beneath the world's most extended ice sheet, which not only conceals its topography, but has also influenced its evolution. It is difficult to apply the term "continent" to what at first glance appears to be simply a huge mass of ice, with no forests, no rivers, no lakes, and only a few and limited forms of life; nonetheless Antarctica is one of the most ancient continents and has undergone complex geological processes which effectively determined its geographical location in the southern extreme of the globe. This evolution also corresponded to the development of forms of life able to adapt to its severe environmental conditions and to attain a high degree of specialization in order to survive each evolutionary phase.

In this way, the extreme features of Antarctica have determined its absolute isolation in human and historical terms, preventing the settlement of any native population and creating totally new patterns for man's approach to an emerged land. Antarctica is the only continent which remained unknown to man for such a long period; only 200 years ago did a spirit of adventure and scientific curiosity attract the first explorers in search of a legendary land, believed to exist only in ancient myths. Once the existence of Antarctica was confirmed, however, its unique environment restricted access for most human purposes and this situation has remained fundamentally unchanged in spite of the recent technological progress which has eased man's occupation of the continent and his related political, economic and scientific activities, but which has not modified its extreme nature.

Phrases such as "the white desert" or "the last boundary on earth" have often been used to emphasize Antarctica's geographical singularity and, over time, they have acquired an ever greater cultural meaning, first for the physical conquest and then the preservation of the continent as the last untouched land on earth.

Distances between Antarctica and nearest continents

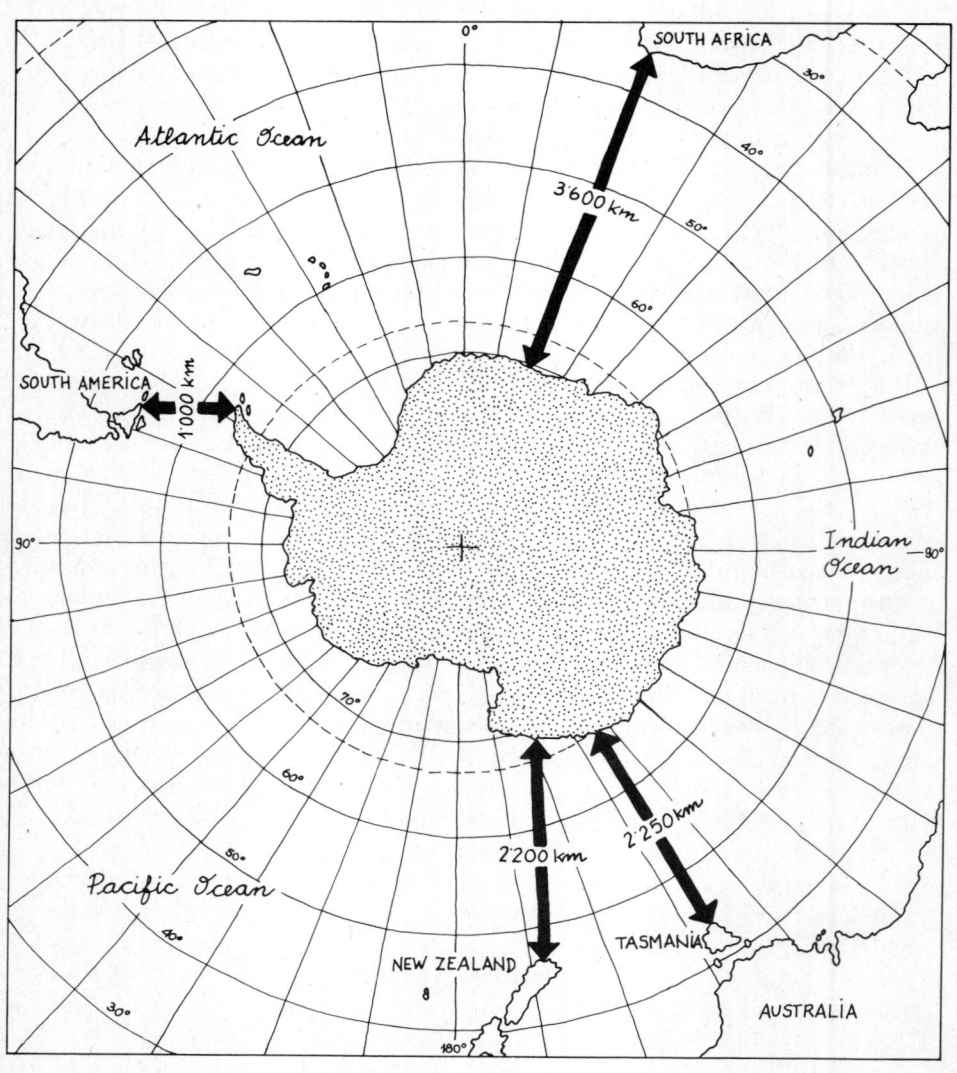

Antarctica

The name Antarctica is often used generically to indicate the ice mass covering the earth's southernmost region, occasionally broken by deglaciated areas and usually surrounded by frozen sea. More specifically, Antarctica, or the Antarctic area, defines a circumpolar region which basically includes two different environments, one continental and the other marine, which are the Antarctic landmass and the oceanic system which surrounds it.

There is not, however, a single definition of its limits. Geographically speaking, no northern territory defines the Antarctic area, as is the case in the Arctic. From a geopolitical point of view, the parallel 60° S is considered as the northern boundary of the region in which most Antarctic legal provisions apply. For scientific purposes a natural parameter has been adopted as the most suitable oceanographical and biological boundary, namely the so-called Antarctic Convergence, the hydrological limit defined by difference in temperature between polar and temperate waters.

Antarctic continent

The Antarctic continental mass covers the furthest edge of the southern hemisphere and, seen from space, it looks like a circular shield of ice centred on the South Pole, outlined by the edge of the ice sheet which covers it. The ice mass does not always coincide with the subglacial topography, but often expands beyond it into the sea. The limit of the continent is, nonetheless, defined by its southernmost surfaces, whether deglaciated land or even floating ice shelves, as the latter are also geographically considered as land.

Isolation

The Antarctic coast has an average distance from the South Pole of 2,500 km, which means that the bulk of the continent lies within the Antarctic Polar Circle (latitude 66°33' S). The sea surrounding the continent, the Antarctic Ocean, separates Antarctica by vast distances from any other emerged land; the closest continent is South America, about 1,000 km distant, while even greater distances separate it from New Zealand (2,200 km), Australia (2,250 km) and South Africa (3,600 km). The geographical isolation of Antarctica is further emphasized by the climatic features of the Antarctic Ocean, one of the coldest, deepest and stormiest, which during winter is covered by a wide layer of marine ice, making access to the continent almost impossible.

Surface

The surface of the Antarctic continent has been estimated at about 14,000,000 km^2, including all ice shelves originating on the continent and flowing into the sea. This figure represents about 1/10 of all emerged lands and is greater than the surface of Europe and Australia, about one third of that of America, and half of Africa. The whole area is almost completely buried beneath the ice and the deglaciated lands emerging from it cover only about 300,000 km^2, just 2% of the total extension.

Average elevation

Another outstanding feature of Antarctica is its average elevation, that is the sum of all its heights divided by its surface. Antarctica is the highest of all continents, with a mean of approximately 2,050 meters above sea level, against a world average of about 600 meters.

The main reason for this significant elevation is the deep layer of ice covering the continent, estimated to average at around 2,000 meters in thickness, though it may exceed 4,000 meters in some areas. Another important factor is the high and extended mountain chains which cross the continent, quite frequently exceeding heights of 4,000-4,500 meters above sea level.

Geographical accidents

The Antarctic continent appears basically round in shape, but a closer observation reveals some major irregularities. One of them is the Antarctic Peninsula, a large S-shaped landmass situated between longitudes 55° W and 75° W. It is the northernmost extremity of Antarctica and the closest to any other continent; due to its relatively easy access from South America, the Peninsula was important in the past as an entry point to Antarctica for sealers, whalers and explorers, and is still today the area with the highest concentration of scientific stations.

Other major irregularities are two large bays, the first in the Weddell Sea (between longitudes 20° W and 60° W) and the second in the Ross Sea (between longitudes 150° W and 170° E). In both regions,the huge mass of ice sliding down from the continent has formed imposing ice shelves, which almost completely conceal the bays: the Filchner and Ronne Ice Shelves in the Weddell Sea, and the Ross Ice Shelf in the Ross Sea.

The 4 poles

When talking of the South Pole as the centre of Antarctica, the reference is to the Geographical South Pole; however, four different points definable as Poles may be identified in Antarctica:

The *Geographical South Pole* corresponds to the point at which the earth's rotation axis passes through the southern hemisphere. It represents the southernmost latitude (90° S), at which all meridians meet.

The *Magnetic South Pole* is the point at which all the lines of force of the earth's magnetic field converge. As the magnetic field is not constant, the position of this pole varies accordingly; it is at present located in the Adelie Land region and its annual displacement is approximately 10-20 km.

The *Geomagnetic South Pole* indicates the position of the Magnetic Pole taking the earth to be a homogeneous magnet; it is thus a theoretical definition used to analyze the variations in the earth's magnetic field. It is located at latitude 78°05' S and longitude 111° E.

The *Pole of Relative Inaccessibility* is the innermost point of the continent and thus the most distant from any coast. It is located at latitude 82°06' S and longitude 54°58' E, 3,720 meters above sea level.

The poles

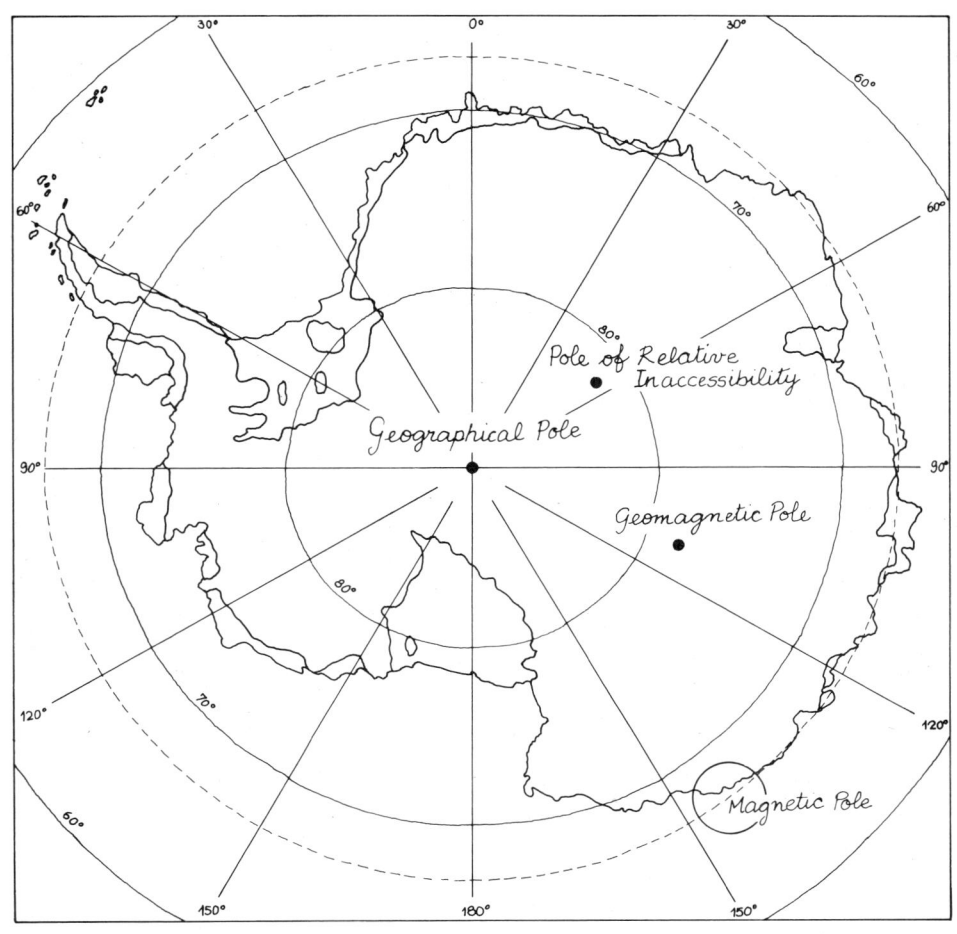

The Antarctic Convergence

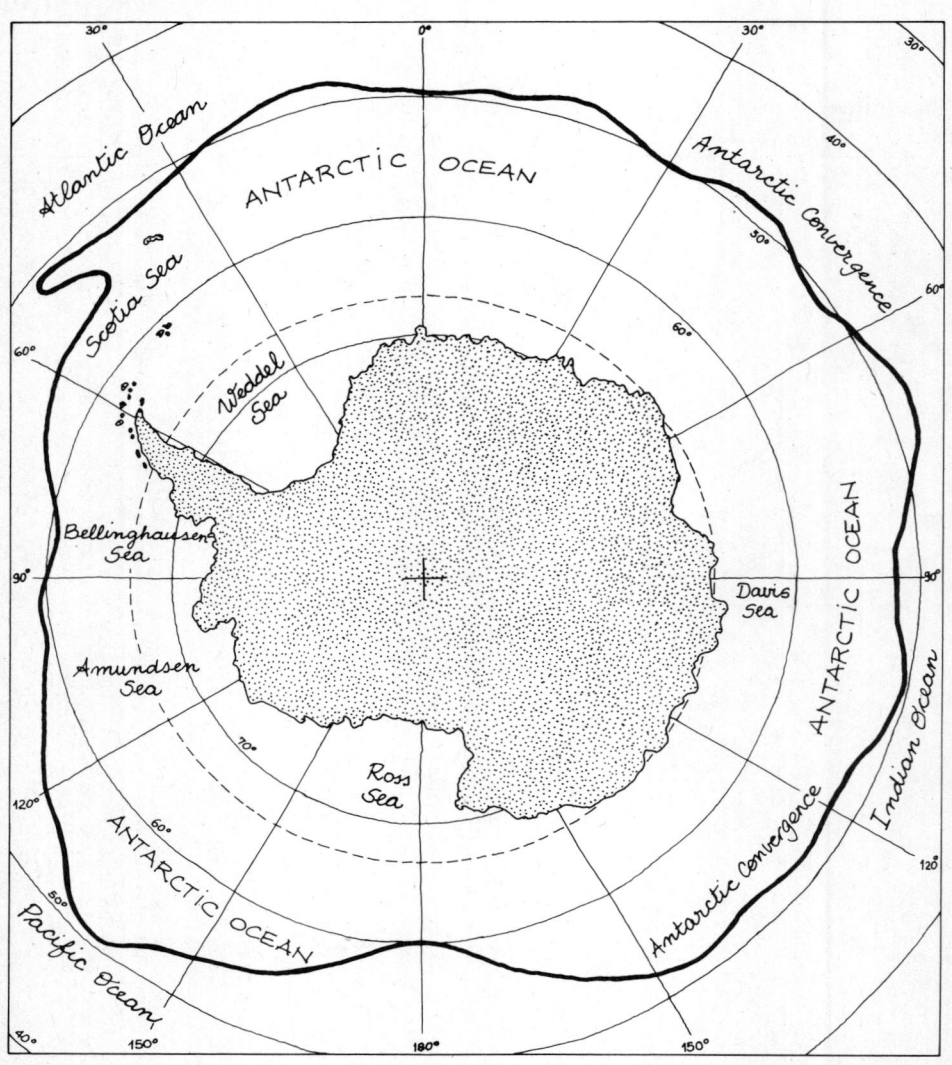

Antarctic Ocean

The Antarctic continent is surrounded by the Antarctic Ocean which forms the southern extremity of the world's three largest oceans, the Pacific, the Atlantic and the Indian, but which, due to very particular physical and chemical characteristics, constitutes a well-defined and separate marine system in itself. It is distinctive for its very high productivity, with low temperatures and a high mineral salt content resulting in the development of the great variety of micro-organisms which form the first level of the Antarctic marine ecosystem.

The Antarctic Ocean covers a total area of approximately 36,000,000 km^2, almost 10% of all the world's seas. It is the only ocean which faces the three largest oceanic systems and, consequently, plays a major role in governing oceanic circulation in the southern hemisphere.

Antarctic Convergence

Its southern limit coincides with the Antarctic coast, while its northern boundary is defined by an imaginary line running between latitudes 50° S and 60° S, known as the Antarctic Convergence. This is the area where the cold and barely saline waters flowing north from the Antarctic coast are pushed downwards by warmer and more saline waters flowing from temperate regions. Apart from being an oceanographical limit, the Antarctic Convergence is also a biological frontier; to its south, all forms of life are adapted for survival in a very specialized environment, forming a well-defined and separate marine ecosystem.

Subantarctic area

In the area surrounding the Antarctic Convergence there are a great number of small islands and archipelagos, scattered at the limits of the Pacific, Atlantic and Indian Oceans. Unlike the Antarctic region, this circumpolar zone does not form a uniform unit and is usually referred to as the subantarctic area, indicating that although it is directly related to the Antarctic environment, particular climatic, biological and oceanic features make it a separate ecosystem.

Among the most important groups of islands there are: on the Atlantic side, the South Georgia, South Sandwich, Tristan da Cunha and Bouvet Islands; on the Indian side, the Prince Edward, Crozet, Kerguelen, Amsterdam, Saint Paul, McDonald and Heard Islands; and on the Pacific side, the Macquarie, Auckland, Campbell, Antipodes and Bounty Islands. These islands are so dispersed and separated by distances so great that they do not alter the extreme isolation of Antarctica.

CHAPTER 2

Origins of Antarctica and some geological aspects

Continental drift

At the beginning of this century a new approach tending towards a more dynamic vision of the earth's evolution emerged in the field of geology and, in this climate of scientific expansion, Wegener, a German scientist, developed the theory of continental drift. According to Wegener's theory, the continents did not always occupy their current position, but drifted as floating islands on a semifluid sublayer and several hundred million years ago were joined to form a single landmass, called Pangea.

Plate tectonics

As a result of further paleomagnetic and oceanic research, Wegener's theory was corrected and updated in the '60s to form the present theory of plate tectonics. The earth's crust, or most external layer, is believed to consist of about a dozen plates, both continental and oceanic, called lithospheric plates. They rest on a layer of semifluid substance called astenosphere, which acts as a kind of conveyor belt allowing the relative displacement of the plates. This phenomenon appears to be induced by convective streams in the astenosphere, the circulation of which is governed by ascendent and descendent trends.

All continental and oceanic plates are in continuous movement and their relationship follows three basic patterns:

a) two plates move towards each other and one is pushed underneath the other (subduction);

b) two plates move away from each other (divergent plates);

c) two plates in contact with each other move in opposite directions on the same plane (transform faults).

In general terms, these movements along the zones of contact of the plates lead to tectonic instability and orogenic phenomena, such as the formation of continental mountain ranges, and oceanic ridges and trenches.

Origins of Antarctica

As far as Antarctica is concerned, this theory has been confirmed by scientific research; it is believed that the Antarctic continent constituted one of the oldest units of a much larger landmass and that its position on the earth has varied through past geological periods.

Reconstruction of Gondwanaland

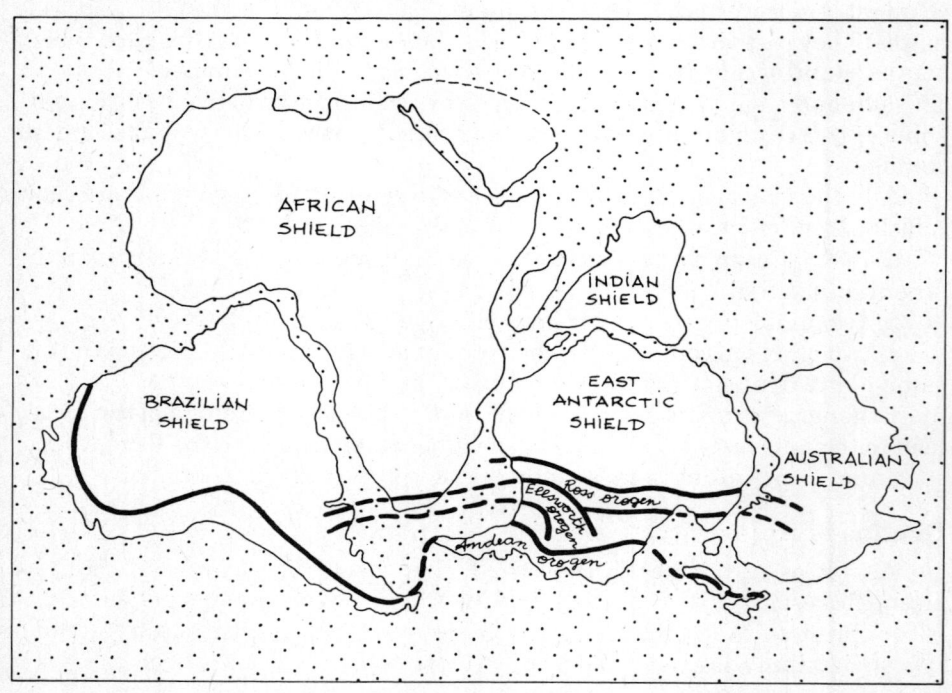

This hypothesis is based on the discovery in Antarctica of fossils of plants (ferns and beech trees) and vertebrates (reptiles and amphibians) common to Africa, India and South America. There is also evidence of similarity between geological structures in Antarctica and Australia, Africa and South America, and glacier traces in all continents that can only be explained by the existence of a common continental mass.

Gondwanaland

It has been possible to determine that in the lower Paleozoic (between 570 and 410 million years ago), all emerged lands were joined together in one continent known as Pangea (from the Greek: *pan* = all and *gea* = lands). In the upper Paleozoic (between 410 and 250 million years ago), Pangea split into two large landmasses: Antarctica, together with South America, Africa, India, Madagascar and Australia formed the continent called Gondwanaland, whereas North America and Eurasia formed the continent called Laurentia.

This is believed to have influenced global atmospheric and oceanic dynamics, determining the conditions for a long glacial period. Between 320 and 230 million years ago, Gondwanaland was covered by a large ice sheet, which appears to have created an effect of gravitational instability causing its drift towards more temperate regions; at the beginning of the Mesozoic (250 million years ago), the continent had already moved away from the influence of the ice.

On the basis of geological evidence, it is believed that approximately 220 million years ago Gondwanaland began to undergo a fragmentation process which, in different geological periods, resulted in the formation of the present continents. The complete separation of Antarctica from other territories, Australia the last, occurred about 65 million years ago during its drift towards the South Pole. This also corresponded with the beginning of a new glacial period which created the conditions for the formation of the Antarctic ice sheet, dating from approximately 20-25 million years ago.

Subglacial topography

The existence of the huge mass of ice which almost completely conceals the continent led to the belief that Antarctica was a uniform landmass. In the last few decades, however, geological and geophysical studies have traced the real topography of the subglacial lands; it is now known that if all the ice were removed, Antarctica would be revealed as two different structures, separated by a basin extending from the Weddell to the Ross Seas, over which the ice has built a solid bridge.

The territory on the eastern side (in relation to the Greenwich meridian), is called East Antarctica and is formed by a single continental plate, round in shape and very old in origin, which represents the nucleus of the original continent.

On the other side, West Antarctica has a much smaller surface area and consists of several island groups of different sizes separated by straits and

Subglacial topography of Antarctica

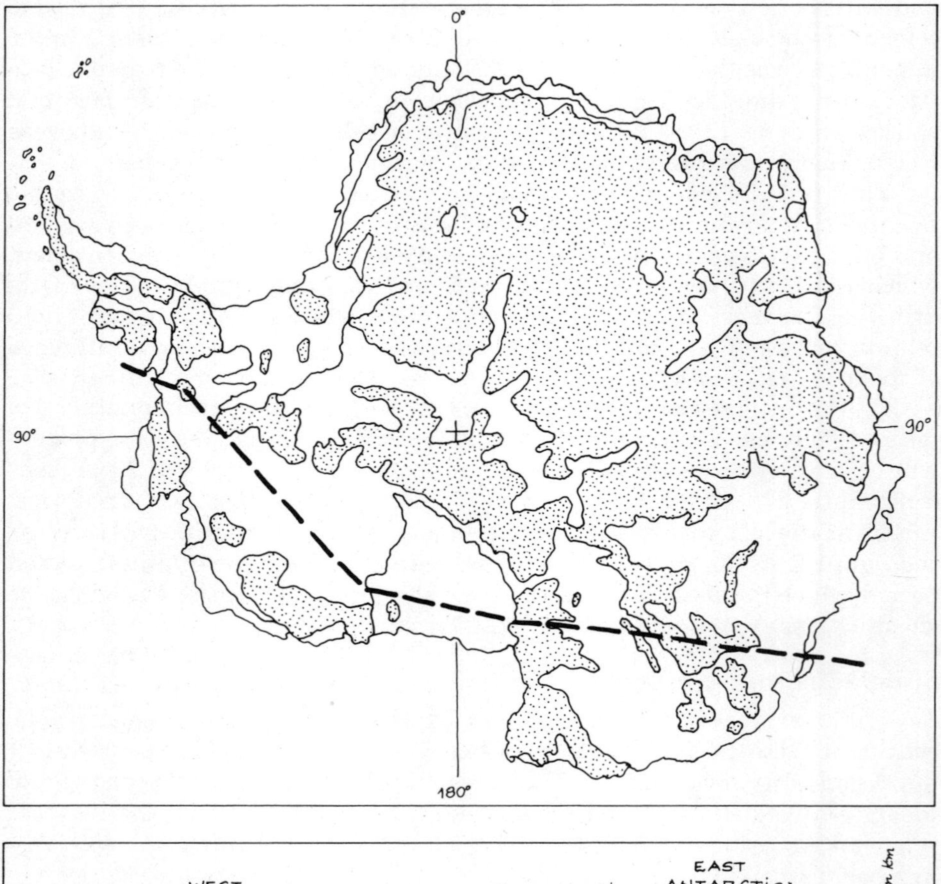

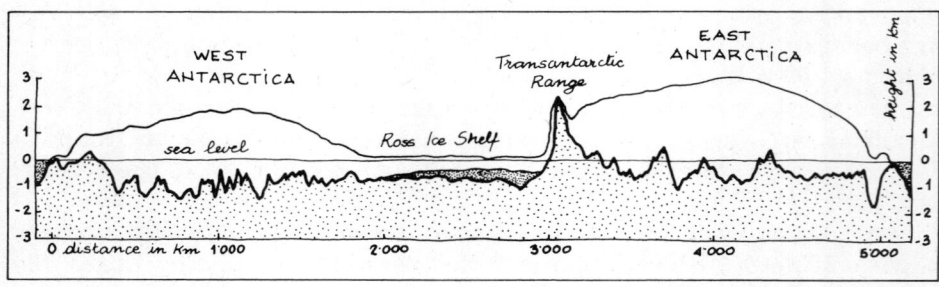

closed seas. It originally formed part of the mountain system running along the southern limit of the Pacific Ocean, which was broken up south of Tierra del Fuego during Gondwanaland's fragmentation to form the so-called Scotia Arch (South Shetland, South Orkney, South Sandwich and South Georgia Islands) and the Antarctic Peninsula. The Peninsula's geological structure is closely related to the South American Andean Range formation, which is why its mountain system is called the Antarctic Andean Range.

Average elevation

An outstanding feature of the deglaciated surface is its average elevation, which in contrast to the ice sheet is relatively low. In East Antarctica the average height is very close to sea level, while in West Antarctica it is approximately 400 meters below sea level, apparently the result of the weight of the ice mass lying over the continent, which according to the isostatic hypothesis would lower the land by an average of about 600 meters.

Continental shelf

This depression can also be observed in the Antarctic continental shelf, the area of relatively low water surrounding the continent. Its average depth is greater than in other regions and varies between 500-800 meters against a world average of 200 meters. The Antarctic continental shelf is usually narrow (30 km against a mean average of 70 km) and surrounds the continent in a regular sweep, except on the eastern side of the Antarctic Peninsula in front of the Weddell Sea, where it is more extended.

Relief of East Antarctica

A major part of the subglacial territory of East Antarctica consists of a flat plateau of low height, completely buried beneath the ice sheet, which in this area reaches its maximum volume. The area is delineated by several mountain systems, with peaks emerging from the ice often exceeding 3,000 meters.

The most extended system is undoubtedly the Transantarctic Range, which consists of several chains crossing the continent from Coats Land on the Weddell Sea up to Victoria Land on the Ross Sea. It passes roughly 500 km from the South Pole and can be taken as the division between the two parts of the continent. With a width of 200-400 km, this range extends for approximately 4,000 km and forms its highest peaks in the Ross area, where imposing glaciers flow down to feed the Ross Ice Shelf. The highest mountain is Mt. Kirkpatrick at around 4,500 meters.

Apart from the Transantarctic Range, other mountain systems delimit the central plateau, especially along the coast between longitude 0° and 70° E; here, several chains run for many thousands of kilometers, with heights varying between 2,500 and 3,500 meters. In Queen Maud Land, the tallest chains are the Muhlig Hofmann, Wohlthat, Humboldt, Sør Rondane and Yamato Mountains; the Prince Charles Mountains along the Mac Robertson Coast is the last mountain system in the coastal area.

Main mountain systems in Antarctica

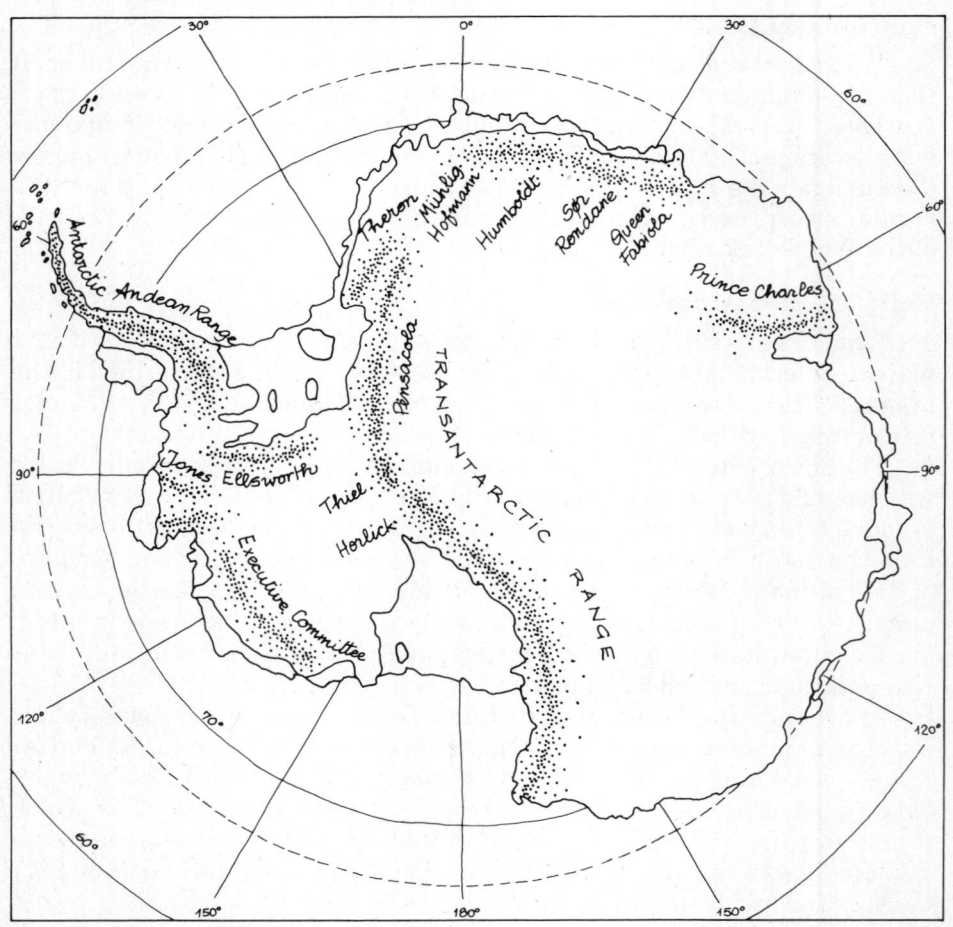

Relief of West Antarctica

The relief of West Antarctica is completely different from that of the eastern territory and does not form one uniform landmass. It is rather an irregular complex of islands which can be seen as a system of mountain chains separated by deep valleys, often below sea level. The most important range in the region is the Antarctic Andean Range, which runs along the Antarctic Peninsula up to the coast of Byrd Land for several thousand kilometers, often exceeding 4,000 meters in height. In this area great differences in land level are found; the lowest point of depression is about 2,500 meters below sea level, giving total elevations of almost 7,000 meters.

Another important mountain system in the region is the Ellsworth Mountains, situated along the coast of the Weddell Sea between the two main mountain ranges of the continent, and including Antarctica's highest peak, Mount Vinson, at 5,140 meters.

Deglaciated areas

The uniformity of the Antarctic landscape is occasionally broken by deglaciated areas which represent an overall 2% of its total surface. They are often found in coastal regions, though a few ice-free zones can also be found in inland areas. Well-known are the so-called *nunataks*, a word of Eskimo origin indicating isolated rocky peaks emerging from the ice sheet.

Other striking features of Antarctic topography are the few deglaciated valleys known as Antarctic oases because of their particularly favorable climate. The most extensive are the Dry Valleys, situated in the Ross coastal zone in the foothills of the Transantarctic Range, where the arid and desert-like soil is covered by sand and is occasionally broken by water streams and small lakes.

Volcanos

In the past intense volcanic activity has been a characteristic of the geological evolution of the continent, especially along its periphery, between East and West Antarctica, and along the Scotia Arch. Although volcanic activity has decreased substantially, a dozen volcanos scattered throughout the region are still active. Among the most important in the Transantarctic area is Mount Erebus on Ross Island, more than 5,000 meters in height. Other active volcanos are located in Byrd Land and in the Antarctic Peninsula area, as well as in the surrounding archipelagos, among them the Deception Island volcano (South Shetlands) and Mount Curry (South Sandwich Islands).

Geological evolution

The geological evolution of Antarctica's eastern and western territories has not been uniform or concurrent.

East Antarctica is the ancient nucleus of the continent and consists of magmatic and metamorphic rocks, the oldest dating from more than 2,500 million years ago, which have consolidated to form a stable crystalline shield.

Geological periods

Period			Million years ago
CENOZOIC	Quaternary	Holocene	0 - 0.01
		Pleistocene	0.01 - 1.6
	Tertiary	Pliocene	1.6 - 5.3
		Miocene	5.3 - 23
		Oligocene	23 - 36.5
		Eocene	36.5 - 53
		Paleocene	53 - 65
MESOZOIC	Cretaceous		65 - 135
	Jurassic		135 - 205
	Triassic		205 - 250
UPPER PALEOZOIC	Permian		250 - 290
	Carboniferous		290 - 355
	Devonian		355 - 410
LOWER PALEOZOIC	Silurian		410 - 438
	Ordovician		438 - 510
	Cambrian		510 - 570
PALEOPROTEROZOIC			570 - 1000
MESOPROTEROZOIC			1000 - 1600
NEOPROTEROZOIC			1600 - 2500
ARCHEAN			over 2500

Towards the end of the Paleoproterozoic period the first orogenic processes, or mountain formation, began in the area of the present Transantarctic Range. The resulting reliefs were later eroded and the region was covered by an inland sea, in which a thick layer of sedimentary material was gradually deposited. During the Cambrian this sedimentary basin was affected by folding which resulted in the Ross Orogen, a cycle accompanied by metamorphism and intrusion of magma of granite origin.

After a period of relative stability characterized by erosion, this region was covered at approximately the end of the Paleozoic period by sand, silt and conglomerate deposits which formed a sedimentary layer known as the Beacon Serie, about 1,500 meters thick. The fossils of fresh water fish, reptiles and vegetation of the genera *Glossopteris* found in its strata confirmed the hypothesis that the continent was, at that time, located in a temperate region.

In the Jurassic a phase of tectonic activity resulted in magmatic intrusions through the sedimentary layer and the formation of column-like structures still visible today. From this point East Antarctica suffered no major geological disturbances, only a few adjustments.

The history of West Antarctica on the other hand is much more recent (dating from about 200-250 million years ago), though it appears that in Precambrian times both parts of the continent shared a similar geological evolution. In general, from its ancient origins up to the present, this region has undergone continual processes of magmatic and tectonic activity followed by folding and deformation, in net contrast to the horizontal formation of East Antarctica.

The presence of metamorphic and plutonic rocks on the West side indicates the deformation process which occurred during the lower Paleozoic. It is likely that the Ellsworth Orogen was the result of conditions of high mobility between the upper Paleozoic and lower Mesozoic. The Triassic and Jurassic were characterized by relative tectonic calm and the temperate conditions of the environment allowed the development of dense flora and an abundance of fauna.

The Jurassic ended with renewed volcanic activity of great intensity anticipating the Andean Orogen and was then followed by a phase of sedimentation and deformation. During the Cretaceous the most relevant geological phenomenon was undoubtedly the Andean Intrusive Phase, which resulted in the formation of the Antarctic Andean Range. It appears that the formation of the Scotia Arch was almost simultaneous and came about as a result of the subduction movement of the southern Pacific plate towards the East, which caused the separation of West Antarctica from South America.

After a period of sedimentation the landmass was subject to intense volcanic activity during the Tertiary, which continued with great intensity until the Pleistocene, resulting in widespread orogenic processes.

CHAPTER 3

A continent of ice
Antarctic glaciology

Nature of ice

Antarctica is often described as a land of ice, but a basic distinction needs to be made between its continental and marine ice.

Continental ice results from the accumulation of snow on the Antarctic landmass which, through several stages, turns into ice. The vast ice sheet resting on the continent slides down towards the coast, often hiding its outline; in certain areas its volume and pressure are so great that it encroaches on the sea for hundreds of kilometers, forming ice shelves from which ice blocks break away to become drifting icebergs.

Conversely, during winter months the cold waters of the Antarctic Ocean can reach temperatures so low that the upper layer of the sea freezes; the result is the formation of marine or pack ice which surrounds the continent, imprisoning icebergs and ice shelves and substantially increasing the total iced surface with no visible interruption.

Formation of continental ice

Continental ice has its origin in the transformation process undergone by snow which accumulates on the ground. The light crystals of recently fallen snow contain a high proportion of air and their density is about 0.05 g/cm^3, but as they touch each other, the pressure of their contact produces heat and causes their edges to melt. The snow crystals thus assume a granular shape and form a much denser mass; this transformation facilitates the further contact of the crystals, their partial melting and their recrystallization into firn, corresponding to the stage at which density varies at about $0.4\text{-}0.6 \text{ g/cm}^3$. As the firn continues to lose interstitial air and the crystals adhere more firmly to each other, the mass becomes more compact and transparent and finally reaches the state of glacier ice, with a density of 0.85 g/cm^3.

Ice movement

Ice is a dynamic substance and its movement is governed by three fundamental conditions, namely the thickness, temperature and surface slope of an ice mass.

First, ice has the property of plasticity, or the capacity to deform under pressure and to maintain its deformed shape once the pressure has ceased; thus, due to the force of gravity, the thickness of an ice mass influences its plastic deformation as a result of the pressure exerted by the ice above.

Second, the temperature of a glacier mass is related to its pressure melting point, that is the reaching of melting temperature due to pressure. Generally, when a glacier is at the pressure melting point, its movement is eased by the presence of meltwaters which allow the mass to slide along its base (as in the case of temperate glaciers). Conversely, if the temperature is below the pressure melting point, the ice mass is sealed to its sublayer and movement occurs mainly as a result of internal deformation of the ice (as in the case of polar glaciers).

Third, the direction of the movement is influenced by the shape of the ice mass which tends to flow towards the maximum surface slope, usually coinciding with the slope of the subglacial relief.

These three elements together determine the velocity of a glacier mass. Velocity is not a constant factor but varies according to morphological and environmental features; it does, however, show a general tendency to increase along the central flowing line rather than along the sides of the ice mass, and at the surface rather than towards the base.

Ice movement

One of the consequences of the uneven movement of a glacier mass is the formation of crevasses, breaks in the ice surface caused by the stress of displacement. They may vary from small to large fractures, their shape and dimension depending on ice velocity. Crevasses have an important function in controlling the infiltration and circulation of meltwaters.

Ice mass balance

In order to better understand ice dynamics, it is necessary to consider ice movement in the broader context of a balance between the total gain, or accumulation, and the total loss, or ablation, of material in a glacier mass.

The gain of material occurs in the accumulation zone, the area situated above the line of permanent snow, where the snow which has fallen throughout the year is transformed into ice; in other words it is the feeding source of the ice mass.

The ablation zone is situated below the accumulation zone and is the area in which the glacier mass experiences a loss of volume because of evaporation, melting, or calving (loss of ice blocks, as in the case of icebergs).

The boundary between the accumulation and ablation areas is called the equilibrium line, and the relationship between the volume of material gained and lost gives the mass balance of a glacier. A period of successive positive mass balances (accumulation greater than ablation) results in an increase in the total ice volume and thus a glacier advance; conversely, successive negative mass balances (accumulation less than ablation) cause a decrease in the total ice volume and therefore a glacier retreat.

Ice mass classification

Reference has so far been made to an ice mass in general terms, but according to morphological features such as shape, size and location, it is possible to classify different kinds of ice structures.

A first distinction may be made between glaciers and ice sheets. The former are ice masses which flow following the subglacial relief, usually contained between valley walls; the latter, instead, completely submerge the pre-glacial relief and expand independently from the underlying topography.

Glaciers

The main subdivision of glaciers includes:

- *Cirque glacier*: an ice mass which occupies a depression;
- *Alpine valley glacier*: a cirque glacier which expands down-valley;
- *Outlet valley glacier*: similar to the latter but fed by an ice sheet;
- *Piedmont glacier*: a valley glacier which expands onto lowlands.

Ice sheets

Among the ice sheets there are:

- *Ice cap*: glacier accumulation situated on an upland surface at a relatively high altitude;
- *Ice sheet*: similar to the above but of greater extension and volume. The earth's only ice sheets are those situated in Antarctica and Greenland.

Origins of the Antarctic ice sheet

The causes of the huge accumulation of ice over Antarctica are still not completely understood, though it is considered that they are strictly related to the drift of the continent to its present position, as well as to past global climatic changes. What is almost certain is that the ice sheet began to form on the eastern side of the continent about 20-25 million years ago, after Antarctica had moved away from temperate regions.

After several phases of glacier advance and retreat, the modern glacial era in Antarctica began with the glacial period, which also affected other continents datable to the Pliocene (about 5 million years ago). At that time the ice sheet reached its maximum extension and then began to withdraw to its present position.

Ice sheet volume

The volume of the Antarctic ice sheet has been calculated by multiplying the continental surface by the average thickness of the ice. The resulting figure of approximately 28,000,000 km^3 represents 90% of all the ice on earth and 68% of world reserves of fresh water; in other words, if the ice sheet were to melt completely, all oceans would rise to roughly 70 meters above their present level.

Ice sheet distribution

The ice sheet is not evenly spread over the continent. Its average thickness is about 2,000 meters, but in several areas the ice expands below sea level and in some can exceed 4,700 meters.

West Antarctica is covered by about 1/6 of the total volume of ice, distributed over its irregular subglacial relief. In East Antarctica the ice sheet forms a much more even plateau, occasionally interrupted by *sastrugis*, or accumulations of iced snow eroded by the wind and appearing as serrated mountains.

Ice sheet dynamics

Two important features characterize the Antarctic ice sheet. First, the ice mass rests to a great extent on a horizontal base and, second, it is below the pressure melting point or, in other words, is frozen to its bed. The movement and shape of the ice sheet are therefore mainly determined by the plastic property of the ice. Temperature does not appear to be constant throughout the ice sheet, but is likely to be higher close to the base, where maximum stress occurs as a result of the weight of the mass above.

In general, the movement of the ice sheet is centrifugal and the ice tends to flow from the centre of the continent towards the coast, following the subglacial topography. Ice velocity is not constant throughout the area; in level regions it is quite slow, ranging between 10 and 30 meters per year, while in irregular relief regions, often close to the coast, it increases steadily ranging from 100 to 1,000 meters per year. In the case of ice shelves ice velocity may exceed 1,200 meters per year.

Ice sheet mass balance

As far as the mass balance is concerned, accumulation is favored by very low temperatures which limit ablation. Net snow accumulation varies between 0 and 800 mm water equivalent per year, but the average figure for the whole continent is estimated to be 120-140 mm per year.

As most of the ice mass is below the pressure melting point, the transformation from snow into ice in the accumulation area takes a relatively long time and occurs at depths varying between 50 and 100 meters.

Ablation occurs mostly because of calving from the edges of the ice sheet, from which large pieces of ice break away to form tabular icebergs. The loss of volume is also due to drifting winds which often blow away the snow. Evaporation occurs throughout the year, in particular because of the dryness of the Antarctic atmosphere, whereas melting only occurs locally during summer.

Due to the very recently available data, estimates on the mass balance of the Antarctic ice sheet are extremely cautious; it appears that, in spite of the negative world trend, the ice sheet balance is at present stable.

Ice shelves

The whole drainage system of the ice sheet is directed towards the coast of the continent, where the ice flows into the sea; in some regions the volume

Antarctic ice shelves

Section of an ice shelf

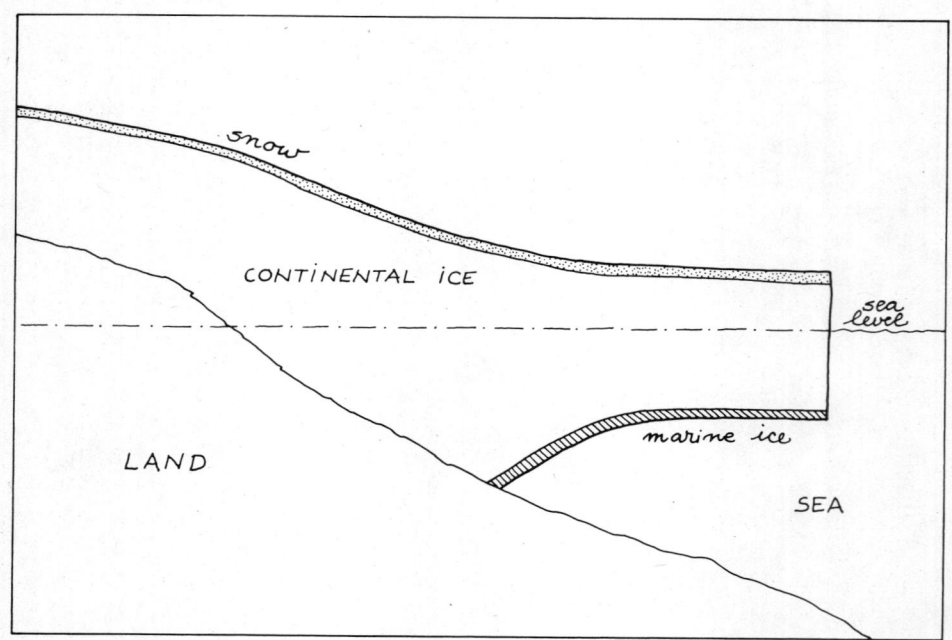

of the discharging mass is so great that it continues expanding and penetrates into the water. The result is the formation of ice shelves, one of the most striking aspects of the Antarctic marine scenery.

The part of the ice shelf closest to the coast is anchored to the underlying relief, while in the sea it floats on the water. Its thickness varies from more than 1,000 meters at its base to about 200 meters at its front, with only 30-40 meters emerging from the sea.

Ice shelves are fed both by the continental ice sheet and the snow which falls on them, as well as by the freezing of the layer of sea water in contact with their lower surface.

They cover almost half of the Antarctic perimeter and represent about 11% of the total surface of the continent (over 1,500,000 km^2). The most extensive are those situated in the Weddell and Ross Seas, the two large bays into which a great part of the ice sheet discharges itself. The largest is the Ross Ice Shelf, with a surface of about 500,000 km^2; in the Weddell Sea, the Berkner Island separates the Ronne Ice Shelf to the west and the Filchner Ice Shelf to the east, together covering a surface of approximately 400,000 km^2. Smaller than the latter are the Larsen, Abbot and Getz Ice Shelves in West Antarctica, and the Shackleton and Amery Ice Shelves in East Antarctica.

Icebergs

From the ice shelves and the glaciers which flow into the Antarctic Ocean, icebergs of different size and shape often break off and drift away from the coast, creating one of the most beautiful features of the Antarctic landscape, but also one of the most dangerous obstacles for navigation.

According to their morphology, icebergs may be separated into two groups. The first includes those which result from calving from glaciers, recognizable by their irregular mountain-like shape; the second includes those produced by the fracture of an ice shelf front, called tabular icebergs, with a flat surface and very steep walls. The majority of Antarctic icebergs are of the tabular kind and can be very large, sometimes exceeding 100 km in width and 200 meters in thickness; only 20-25% of their total volume emerges above the water.

As icebergs are inert floating masses their drift is governed by sea currents and influenced by winds, which can push them as far north as latitude 45°-50° S.

Pack ice

The most extraordinary seasonal change in Antarctica is perhaps the freezing of the Antarctic Ocean. Every year, marine or pack ice alternately invades and frees more than one tenth of the whole surface of the southern hemisphere. The sea begins to freeze at the end of summer and the ice reaches its maximum extension in September, covering a surface of almost 20,000,000 km^2; in about March, it withdraws again to a minimum extension of approximately 3,000,000 km^2.

Maximum and minimum pack ice extension

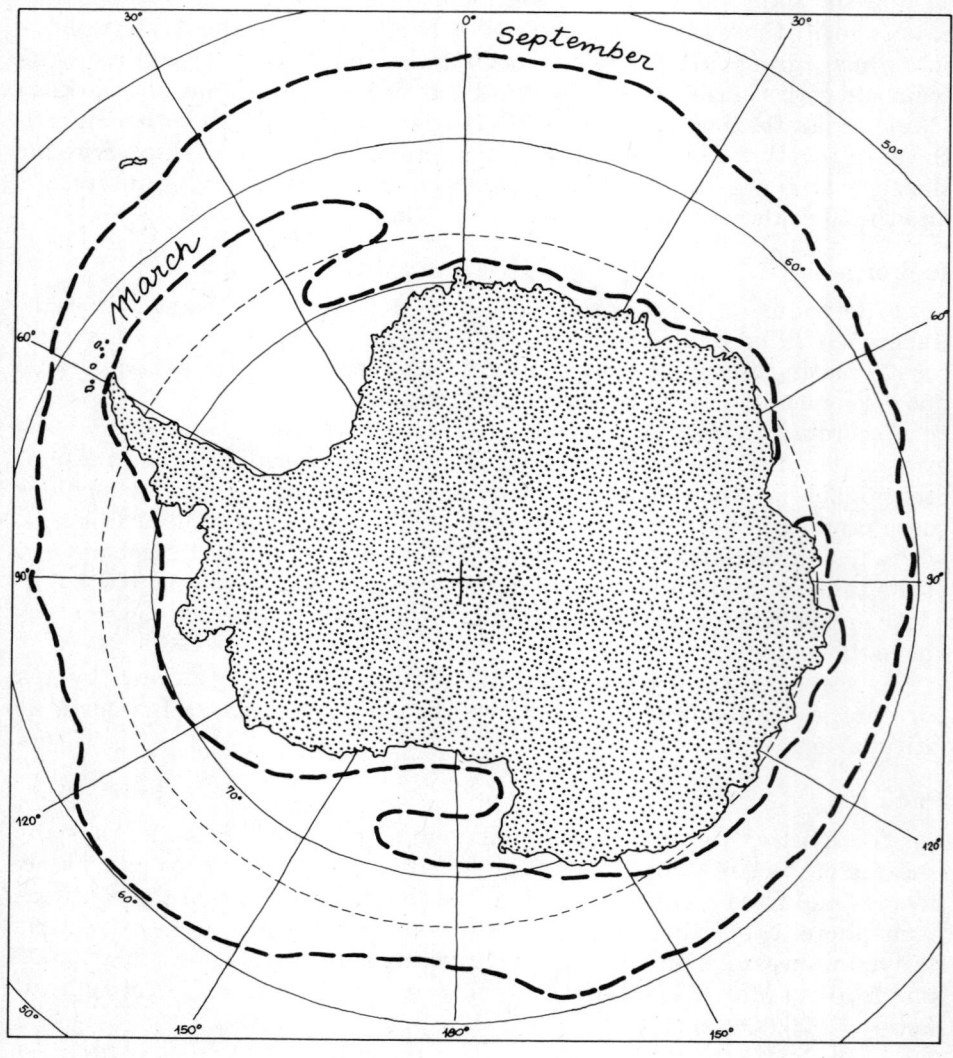

Pack ice starts forming in coastal areas, where small fragments of ice come into contact with each other and slowly form a compact mass which gradually loses salinity and appears as thin round plates. In the course of time, these ice discs become thicker and are pushed together by currents and winds forming larger ice floes, which crush each other, break and join again until they completely cover the sea surface. Drifting icebergs are imprisoned by the pack ice and the whole marine landscape assumes a chaotic aspect.

Pack ice reaches its equilibrium after several years when it is about 3-4 meters thick. The part of the marine ice which remains anchored to the coast is called fast or fixed ice, while the free-floating part is called drift ice. On the frozen sea surface it is sometimes possible to see ice-free areas of different size, called *polynyas*, caused by the effect of the wind on the movement of ice floes.

The annual melting cycle of a large part of the pack ice begins again in late spring. It is a fairly slow process because in spite of the substantial increase in light and temperature, the ice reflects more than 80% of solar radiation back into space. The melting accelerates only when the first meltwaters appear and the ice floes then break apart, decrease in volume and are carried north by wind and sea currents. Drifting pack ice usually melts completely within latitude 60° S.

CHAPTER 4

Climate and atmospheric phenomena

The vast iced surface of Antarctica plays a fundamental role in governing the thermal balance of the whole planet. Since the beginning of the Antarctic glacial era some 20-25 million years ago, Antarctica has represented the cold well of the world's thermodynamic engine; in the long term, it determines the earth's climate, as well as oceanic and atmospheric circulation, influencing in this way all marine and land ecosystems depending on it.

In Antarctica meteorological studies have proved difficult, owing to severe environmental conditions; all research in this field is very recent and has been undertaken systematically only in the last few decades, in particular since the International Geophysical Year of 1957 which marked the starting point of modern Antarctic science.

Solar radiation

Antarctica's climatic conditions, which make it one of the world's most inhospitable regions, are governed by its extreme geographical position. The Antarctic landmass is located around the point at which the earth's rotation axis crosses the globe, which means that the angle of incidence of solar radiation is the widest possible and that the intensity of solar energy is lower than anywhere else in the world (except the Arctic). Further, due to the inclination of the earth's rotation axis as the planet moves around the sun, the total amount of solar radiation is not uniformly distributed throughout the year and the most remarkable seasonal differences can be observed. Summer corresponds to the period of the year when the maximum amount of light is received, whereas during winter the opposite is true.

Solstices

Even in summer, however, the sun describes a very low curve over the horizon and attains its highest point on December 21st during the summer solstice, when the earth's rotation axis reaches its maximum inclination angle of 23°27'. Conversely, the sun reaches its lowest point on the horizon on June 21st, during the winter solstice.

Antarctic Polar Circle

The Antarctic Polar Circle, situated at latitude 66°33' S, represents the line beyond which, during the summer solstice, the sun remains visible over the horizon for the whole day, while during the winter solstice it never appears.

Conditioning factors

Even though during summer the amount of solar radiation received by Antarctica is greater than anywhere else in the world, several factors prevent this energy from being absorbed. The most important of these is the high refraction power of the ice which reflects back into space about 80% of solar radiation, thus causing a substantial loss of heat. Considering the enormous extension of the iced area this phenomenon has a major thermal effect, which becomes even greater during winter because of the formation of pack ice. The dispersion of solar radiation is also determined by the high average elevation of the continent, as well as by the low water content in the Antarctic atmosphere which prevents energy from being absorbed.

Albedo

These are the reasons why the relation between received and reflected radiation, called albedo, is negative throughout the year, even though during summer the sun shines constantly. All these factors determine the extremely rigorous conditions prevailing in Antarctica, much more severe even than in the Arctic.

Atmospheric circulation

Atmospheric circulation over the continent is governed by the presence of a permanent anticyclone located over the polar highlands, which generates a centre of high pressure and thus a very cold and dry climate. As it moves away from the inland area this mass of air gradually loses stability, increasing in humidity and temperature. The result is the formation of depression areas in the circumpolar region between latitudes 60° S and 70° S, where several low pressure centers give rise to cyclones, which are pushed towards the east by strong western winds and carry bad weather with rain and snow.

Temperature

Climatic conditions are in general not uniform over the continent; the temperature tends to decrease moving from the coast towards the inland area. This trend is the result of several factors such as the increase in latitude, the higher average elevation of the polar highlands, and the presence of the landmass.

During summer, the average temperature in coastal regions is about 0°C, while it varies between -15°C and -35°C in inland areas. During the coldest months the temperature along the coast ranges from -15°C to -30°C and in the central plateau from -40°C to -70°C. The lowest temperature of -89,6°C was recorded in 1983 at Vostock Station (USSR) on the polar plateau. In contrast to the rest of the continent, the northwestern part of the Antarctic Peninsula is the only region which enjoys a more temperate climate, with an average winter temperature of about -9°C.

Average annual temperatures in Antarctica (in °C)

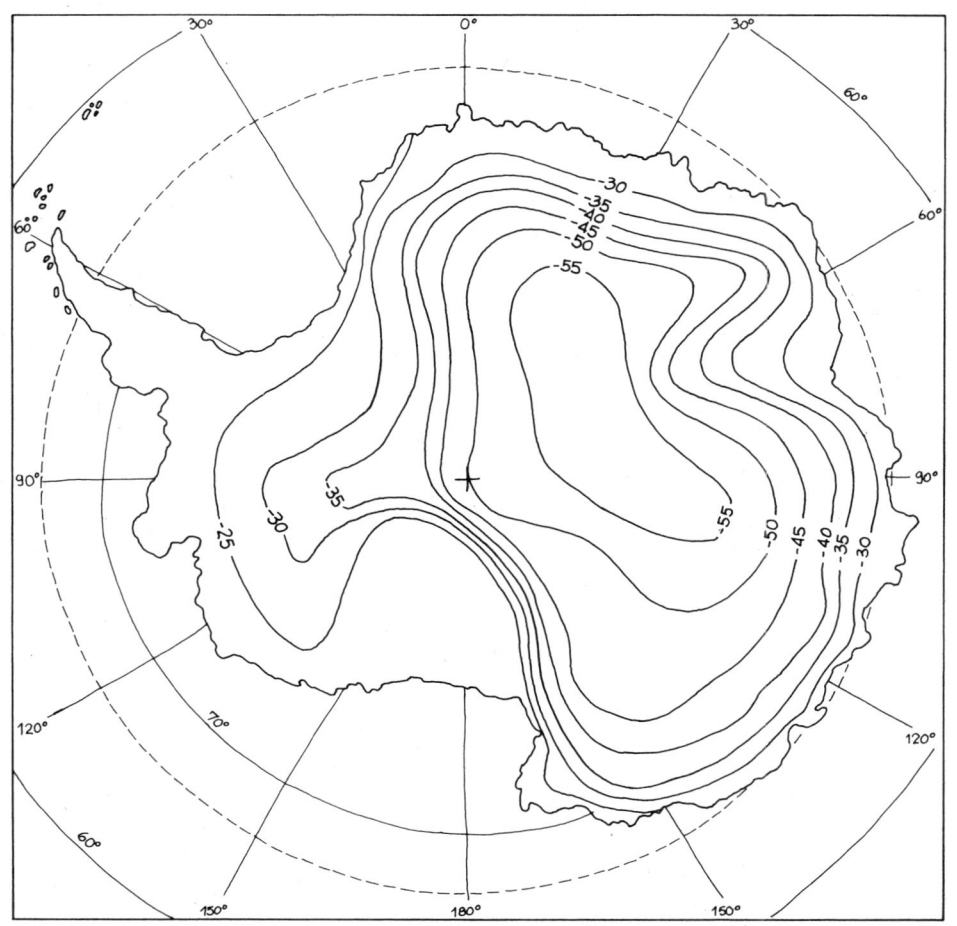

Average annual precipitation in Antarctica (in mm water equivalent)

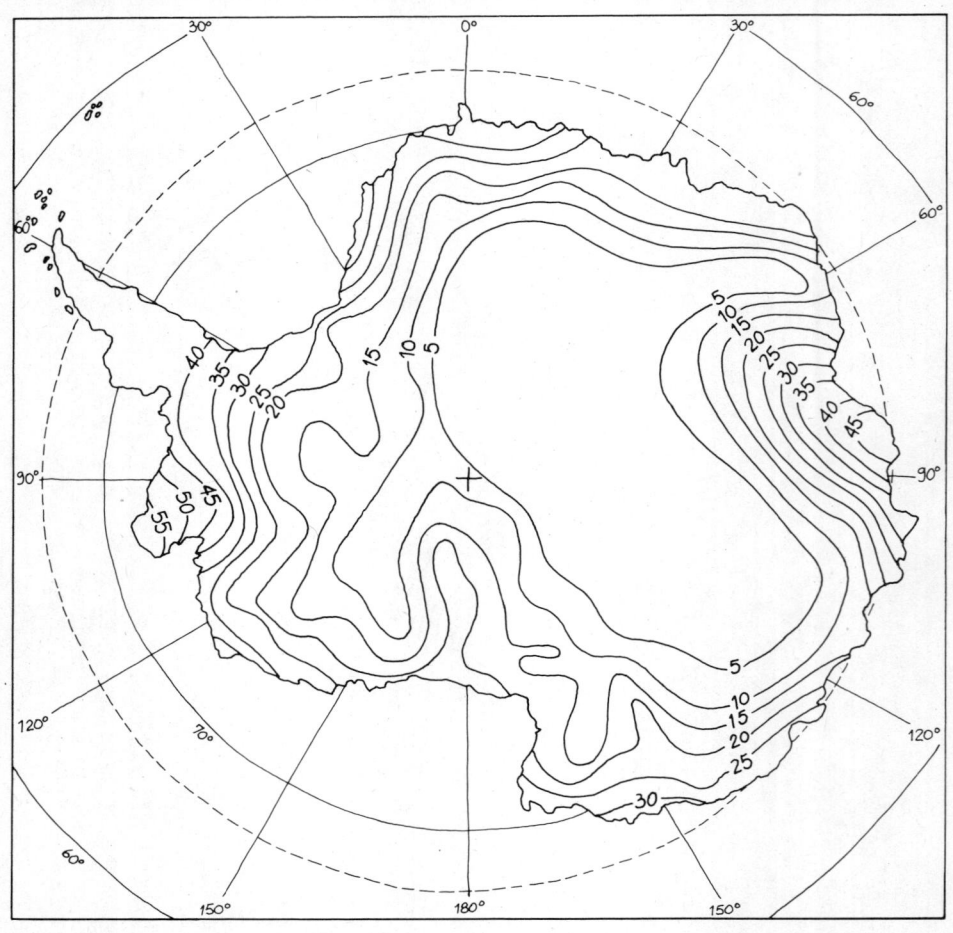

Atmospheric humidity

As a result of the extremely cold temperature, the absolute atmospheric humidity is very low, although the relative humidity is higher. The dryness of the air makes the Antarctic atmosphere extremely pure and transparent, and generally facilitates the ablation (loss of volume) of the glacier mass in the form of evaporation.

Precipitation

One of the consequences of the predominantly dry climate is the relatively light amount of snow falling over the continent, enough however to determine a net accumulation from one year to the next. Parallel to temperature, snowfall tends to decrease moving from the coast towards the inland area, with values ranging between 200 and 800 mm water equivalent per year in the coastal region and falling to negligible values on the polar plateau. In general terms, average snowfall over the continent varies at around 120-140 mm water equivalent per year, one of the lowest figures in the world. The northern part of the Antarctic Peninsula is the only region in which higher levels are reached, and in which it may rain.

Winds

On the central plateau loss of heat from the ice sheet often results in thermal inversion, that is the cooling of the lowest layer of air in contact with the surface. The central anticyclone pushes these masses of extremely cold air towards the coast following the land relief, which decreases in height sharply along the continental edge. One of the main results is the formation of strong east and south-east surface winds, called catabatic winds, which blow with extreme violence over the coast and can reach speeds of 200 km/h. In the inland areas the result is strong blizzards, in which falling snow is mixed by the wind with snow lifted from the ground.

These strong winds, with extremely low temperatures, often create conditions very close to the human tolerance limit and, for this reason, great care has to be taken when preparing for any kind of activity in Antarctica.

Cloudiness

Cloudiness over the continent varies according to season and in particular tends to decrease during winter. This is the result of both lower humidity and the increase in the iced surface due to the formation of pack ice as clouds follow the ice-free water front. Generally, West Antarctica is more overcast than East Antarctica.

Over the polar highlands stratiform clouds at uniform level are predominant, while over the periphery cloudiness is more variable, especially during summer. The oceanic area is characterized by overcast skies, with high levels of average annual cloudiness.

Optical phenomena

The very particular features of the Antarctic atmosphere result in the occurrence of optical phenomena, which are caused by the refraction of light on the water particles contained in the air. Among the most common are: halos, luminous rings around the sun (parhelion) or the moon (paraselene), which cause the illusion of three suns or moons on the same line; mirages, caused by the refraction of light on superimposed layers of cold and warm air; blinding, which results in loss of the notion of visual depth and makes it difficult to locate objects in space.

Auroras

The most extraordinary phenomenon observable in Antarctica, however, is undoubtedly the aurora australis, or southern lights, a luminous effect of incredible beauty resembling dawn. This is a phenomenon of electromagnetic origin which occurs in the high atmosphere, and is the result of the combined effect of the intense magnetic activity close to the pole and the high ionization of the gases in the upper layers of the atmosphere. Auroras may be more easily observed closer to the magnetic pole, but can also be seen in other regions.

Oceanic circulation

Oceanic circulation around Antarctica is basically governed by the Antarctic Circumpolar Current which plays a key role in the interchange of water between the Pacific, Atlantic and Indian Oceans. This current, the result of both the difference in sea water density and wind action, acts as a kind of conveyor belt and flows around the continent from west to east following its submarine topography. Its predominant belt-like circulation is interrupted by deviations in the Weddell and Ross Sea areas, where western gyros of cyclonic origin occur.

The direction west-east of the Antarctic Circumpolar Current also influences the drift of icebergs and ice floes.

CHAPTER 5

Antarctic biology

Conditions in Antarctica are not favorable for the development of complex forms of life, due mainly to the predominantly low temperature, the extremely uneven distribution of light throughout the year, and the presence of the ice sheet covering 98% of the total surface. For these reasons Antarctic flora and fauna are concentrated in coastal and marine areas, where a great part of the deglaciated surface is found and environmental conditions are less severe. The land ecosystem is thus extremely restricted and almost all life systems depend on the sea, which provides the resources for the survival of most species.

Land ecosystem

Deglaciated areas are characterized by the absence of trees, shrubs and grasses and are often covered by a gravelly soil lacking in humus, inhibiting the growth of vegetation. The reduced flora is often associated with the presence of bird rookeries as the mineral substances necessary to plants are provided mainly by organic material of animal origin.

The flora consists for the main part of more than 400 species of lichen, symbiotic organisms composed of algae and fungi which feed on the mineral salts they extract from the rocks through the secretion of acid substances. The group of Bryophytes is also relatively abundant, with about 80 species of moss and 25 species of liverwort. Over 300 species of land and freshwater algae have been identified, as well as a few dozen species of fungi and bacteria. Among the Phanerogams there are only 2 flowering species: the *Deschampsia antarctica* and the *Colobanthus crassifolius*.

The reduced varieties of plants shelter and feed an even smaller community of insects and arachnids. There are no reptiles or true land mammals, and all species belonging to the upper fauna such as seals, penguins and seabirds are considered to belong to the marine ecosystem.

Marine ecosystem

While the land environment only allows the survival of a few isolated communities, the coastal and oceanic environment is, in contrast, extremely rich in plant and animal life and forms a well-structured marine ecosystem, governed by a complex community organization and interdependent relationships. The source of this dynamism is the high productivity of the Antarctic

Antarctic food chain

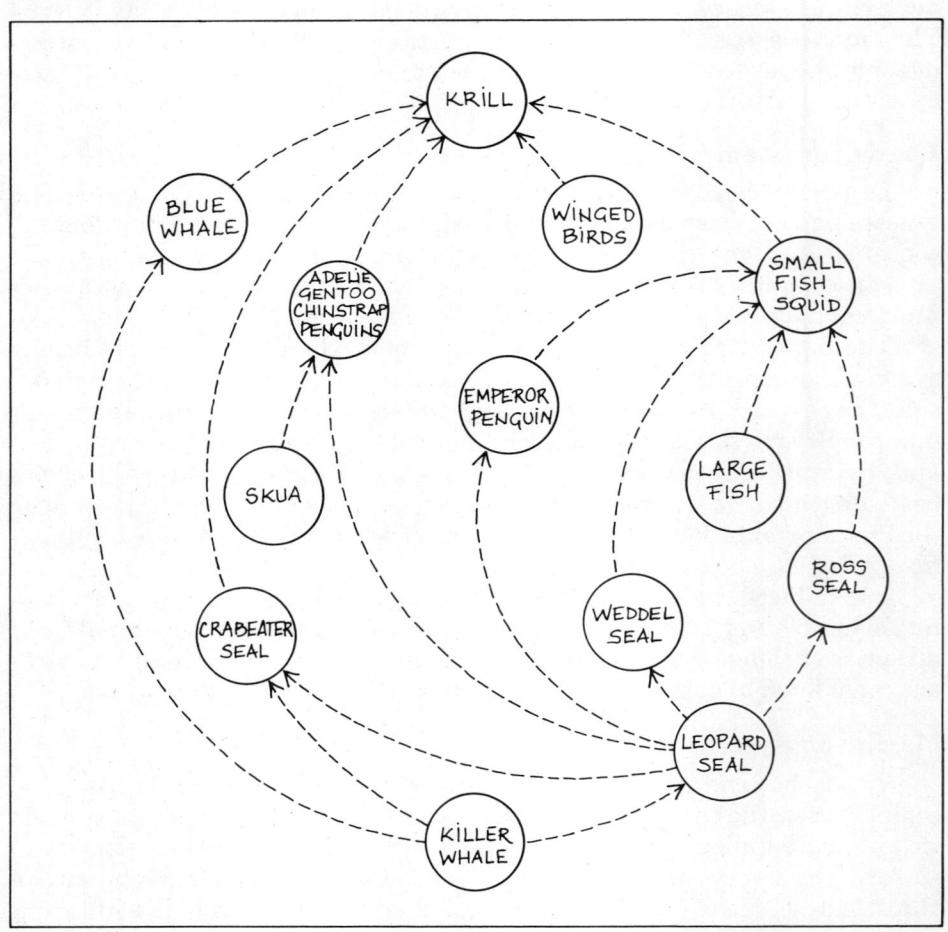

Ocean, in which the Antarctic Circumpolar Current assures the continuous replacement of water carrying heat and nutrients from lower latitudes, as well as a constant renewal of oxygen. The low temperature of the Antarctic Ocean maintains in suspension a high amount of carbon dioxide (CO_2) and oxygen (O_2), essential to the photosynthesis of plant species and the respiration of marine organisms. The water is also enriched by a high mineral salt content, mainly phosphates and nitrates, the movement of which towards the coastal areas is assured by the upward cycle of deep waters.

Plankton

All these conditions allow the proliferation of plankton, the primary produce of the Antarctic Ocean and the lowest stage of the Antarctic food chain. Plankton is a community of free-floating organisms which may be subdivided into phytoplankton (plant organisms) and zooplankton (animal organisms). Their displacement is strictly related to sea currents as they are unable to move on their own, except vertically to get close to or away from light.

Phytoplankton consists of microscopic and mostly unicellular algae and protozoa which feed on energy from the sun; zooplankton is made up of herbivorous animals feeding on phytoplankton, and carnivorous animals feeding on other plankton organisms.

Krill

Among the zooplankton the most dominant group is krill. This word of Norwegian origin meaning "small fish" defines several species of small crustaceans of the family *Euphausiidae*, of which the best-known is the *Euphausia superba*, a shrimp-like animal about 4-6 cm long. Krill lives in enormous swarms about 10-20 meters deep which extend over several hundred meters, with a density occasionally exceeding 15 kg per cubic meter of water. Its capacity to stay in swarms is related to the emission of a green-pale blue luminescence, which allows krill to remain in sight of each other.

Little is known about the population dynamics of these small crustaceans. It appears that krill eggs are laid during summer on the water surface and then sink up to 2,000 meters in depth, where they hatch into microscopic larvae. Moving upwards, they undergo several transformation stages and acquire their adult features when they reach a length of about 10 mm. According to recent research the average life span of krill is around 6-7 years, instead of the 3-4 years estimated previously.

Estimates of the krill biomass (annually renewable) are still only approximate and in spite of early optimistic estimates approaching 1,000 million tons, specialists at present tend to accept more cautious figures varying at around 200-600 million tons. Krill stocks are distributed around the Antarctic continent south of the Antarctic Convergence, with higher density areas in the South American and the Indian sectors.

These small organisms play a key role in the dynamics of the Antarctic marine ecosystem as, in a direct or indirect way, all the upper fauna depends on them; their migrations are followed by the majority of fish, squid, penguins, seabirds, seals and whales, which in turn are followed by their predators. This means that the Antarctic ecosystem is extremely linear and simple, and that the progression from small organisms to large mammals necessarily and almost exclusively occurs through krill.

Invertebrates

The Antarctic Ocean is also inhabited by a large variety of invertebrates such as sponges, coelenterata, annelida, echinoderms (starfish and sea-urchins) and molluscs, of which the most important are squid.

Finfish

About 100 species of finfish breed in the sea south of the Antarctic Convergence, the majority of which belong to the family *Notothenidae*, an example being the Antarctic cod (*Notothenia rossii*) well-known for its commercial value. The ice fish is considered to be of special interest because of its adaptation to the Antarctic iced waters; it is a transparent fish, the blood of which has no haemoglobin, allowing it to maintain viscosity and coagulation at low temperatures.

Marine mammals

Marine mammals and seabirds form the two largest groups of the Antarctic upper fauna, of which the former can be divided into pinnipeds (true seals and fur seals) and cetaceans (whales, dolphins and porpoises).

Pinnipeds (seals)

Pinnipeds are mammals of land origin which have gradually evolved towards a high aquatic specialization, but unlike cetaceans have not completely abandoned the land to which they return to fulfil reproduction and breeding cycles. Apparently the descendants of bears and primitive otters, they have adapted their bodies to their new environment, acquiring a hydrodynamic shape, transforming their limbs into flippers and retracting their external organs.

There are three different groups of pinnipeds: Otarids (sea lions and fur seals), Phocids (true seals) and Odobaenids (walrus), of which the latter are found only in the northern hemisphere. Of the six species of seal living in Antarctica only the Antarctic fur seal belongs to the Otarid family, while the Crabeater, Weddell, Leopard, Ross and Elephant seals belong to the Phocid family. One of the visible features distinguishing Otarids from Phocids is that the former have outer ears and, when on land, are able to move their rear flippers forwards in a quadruped-like way, whereas the latter can only crawl with reptile-like movements.

Seals live all around the Antarctic continent without occupying any specific area, and move either by swimming or on drifting ice floes. They are well adapted to stand cold temperatures through a layer of fat between their fur and muscles, which is also an important energy reserve in case of forced fasts.

One male can impregnate several females and the following gestation period lasts between 8 and 12 months according to species. Adult females usually give birth to one pup per year which is born in spring and has a lactation period varying from 1 to 4 months. Young animals become sexually mature between the 4th and 6th year of age and their average life span ranges from 18 to 24 years. Their predators are the Killer whale and also, for certain species, the Leopard seal.

Antarctic fur seal

The Antarctic fur seal (*Arctocephalus gazella*) is the only Otarid existing in Antarctica. Its fur is dark brown and its coat consists of two different kinds of hair, one long and hard and the other short and soft.

The adult male measures about 1,80 meters and weighs about 140 kg, while the female is usually smaller (1,30 meters and 50 kg). The Antarctic fur seal often gathers in colonies in which each male occupies a territory and forms a harem with several females. The female has a gestation period of 9 months and gives birth to one pup per year, which is born in December and has a lactation period of almost 4 months. The Antarctic fur seal basically feeds on krill, but also on fish and squid.

The breeding range of the Antarctic fur seal is mostly subpolar; it lives in the subantarctic islands close to the Antarctic Convergence, with an important concentration in the South Georgia Islands. Due to the high commercial value of its fur, the Antarctic fur seal has been overexploited in recent centuries and its present population of approximately 1,000,000 is estimated to be much smaller than in the past.

Crabeater seal

The Crabeater seal (*Lobodon carcinophagus*) is considered to have the greatest numbers of any seal species in the world with a population of about 25,000,000. Its demographic expansion seems to be the result of the surplus of food reserves made available by the decline of the whale population.

The female is a little larger than the male, which measures almost 3 meters and weighs 200-250 kg. The color of the fur varies with age, but is predominantly yellow-beige. During the reproduction period the Crabeater seal forms family groups composed of a male, a female and a pup, which is born on the ice floes in spring and has a lactation period of about 4 weeks.

The Crabeater seal usually lives on the edge of the pack ice area and moves according to the seasonal movement of the ice. It feeds almost exclusively on krill and this is why it was given its name by sealers, who thought that krill were little crabs. It has a special filter-like dentition which allows it to take in large amounts of krill, eliminating the water through its lobed teeth. The Killer whale and the Leopard seal are the main predators of the Crabeater seal, particularly the latter which is specialized in the capture of pups and young animals.

The almost exclusive dependence of Crabeater seals on one food resource has recently focused attention on the fact that any significant impact on krill stocks would also result in the alteration of the whole marine ecosystem.

Weddell seal

The Weddell seal (*Leptonychotes weddelli*) is slightly larger than the Crabeater seal; it can be distinguished by the small size of its head in relation to its body and by the light grey color of its fur. The female can be larger than the male, measuring about 3 meters and weighing up to 400 kg.

The Weddell seal is considered to be the world's southernmost mammal as it lives in the heavy pack ice regions close to the coast. It does not migrate towards the north during winter and spends most of its time in the water beneath the ice. The need for air forces it to open holes in the pack ice with its teeth, causing dental problems in adulthood.

The female begins to come onto the surface during October-November to give birth to one pup, the lactation period of which lasts approximately 6 weeks. The growth of the pup is surprisingly fast and it reaches adult size in a few months.

The Weddell seal feeds primarily on fish, especially Antarctic cod, and supplements its diet with squid and crustaceans. The adult is not particularly menaced by predators as it tends to remain in coastal pack ice areas, where access for the Killer whale and the Leopard seal is restricted. Its total population has been estimated at 800,000 and is considered to be stable.

Ross seal

The Ross seal (*Ommatophoca rossi*) is the least known and the rarest of all true seals. It is a solitary animal which lives within the Antarctic Convergence in the medium-density pack ice areas.

The Ross seal measures about 3 meters and weighs around 200 kg, and its fur is grey with lighter spots. It is believed to form family groups like the Crabeater seal and reproduction appears to take place in November. It feeds on squid, fish and krill.

The reason for the rarity of this species is still at present unclear as it has not traditionally been persecuted by sealers and the food surplus left by the decline in the whale population should have contributed to its demographic expansion. The Ross seal population has been estimated at around 150,000-200,000.

Leopard seal

The Leopard seal (*Hydrurga leptonyx*) is perhaps the best-known of all seals, largely for its remarkable predator activity. It is one of the largest pinnipeds, capable of reaching 4 meters in length and 400 kg in weight. It may be recognized by the reptile-like shape of its neck and head, equipped with well-developed jaws and powerful teeth. The color of its fur is dark grey on its back, becoming much lighter on the abdomen with numerous small black spots.

The total population is estimated at about 500,000, the distribution of which varies according to seasonal pack ice movements and to the displacement of food resources. It may occasionally reach subantarctic areas.

The Loepard seal has solitary habits and spends most of its time in the sea. The birth of its pup appears to take place in late spring, with a lactation period of about 4 weeks. The Leopard seal basically feeds on warm-blooded animals, but also on fish, squid and krill. Its diet varies according to seasonal availability: in spring krill appears to be its main diet; at the beginning of summer young Crabeater and Weddell seals become available; and at the end of summer when young penguins go to sea, its activity around penguin colonies becomes more intense. Together with the Killer whale, the Leopard seal is the predator occupying the highest level in the Antarctic food chain.

Elephant seal

The Elephant seal (*Mirounga leonina*) lives further north than all other Antarctic seals and may be considered as a circumpolar inhabitant, scattered throughout all the subantarctic islands, with a high concentration in the South Georgia Islands and an important continental settlement in the Valdez Peninsula (Argentina).

It is the largest of all pinnipeds; an adult male can measure over 5 meters and weigh 3,5 tons, while the female is less than half the size of the male (2,30 meters and 900 kg). The Elephant seal displays an important sexual dimorphism; the male has a prominent snout ending in a proboscis which inflates when it is aroused, particularly during the reproduction period. The Elephant seal is covered by a wrinkled skin with short brown hair, grey in juveniles and almost black in pups.

The Elephant seal forms large colonies in coastal regions, in which the male usually arrives a few weeks before the female and begins ferocious fights to assert its territorial primacy. It has polygamous habits and may form harems composed of many females, while defeated males and juveniles usually settle apart. Pups are born in October-November and their lactation period lasts about 3 weeks.

The Elephant seal basically feeds on squid and fish. Its main natural predator is the Killer whale, but in the past its most merciless enemy has been man, attracted by the high commercial value of its fat. Since the end of sealing, the total population of the Elephant seal has recovered and at present is estimated at 700,000.

Cetaceans (whales)

Cetaceans make up the other large group of marine mammals inhabiting Antarctica. They are not permanent residents, but migrate during winter towards more temperate latitudes in order to carry out reproduction and breeding cycles and return to the Antarctic Ocean in summer attracted by its abundant food stocks.

Cetaceans have completely adapted themselves to their marine environ-

Surface features of some Antarctic whales

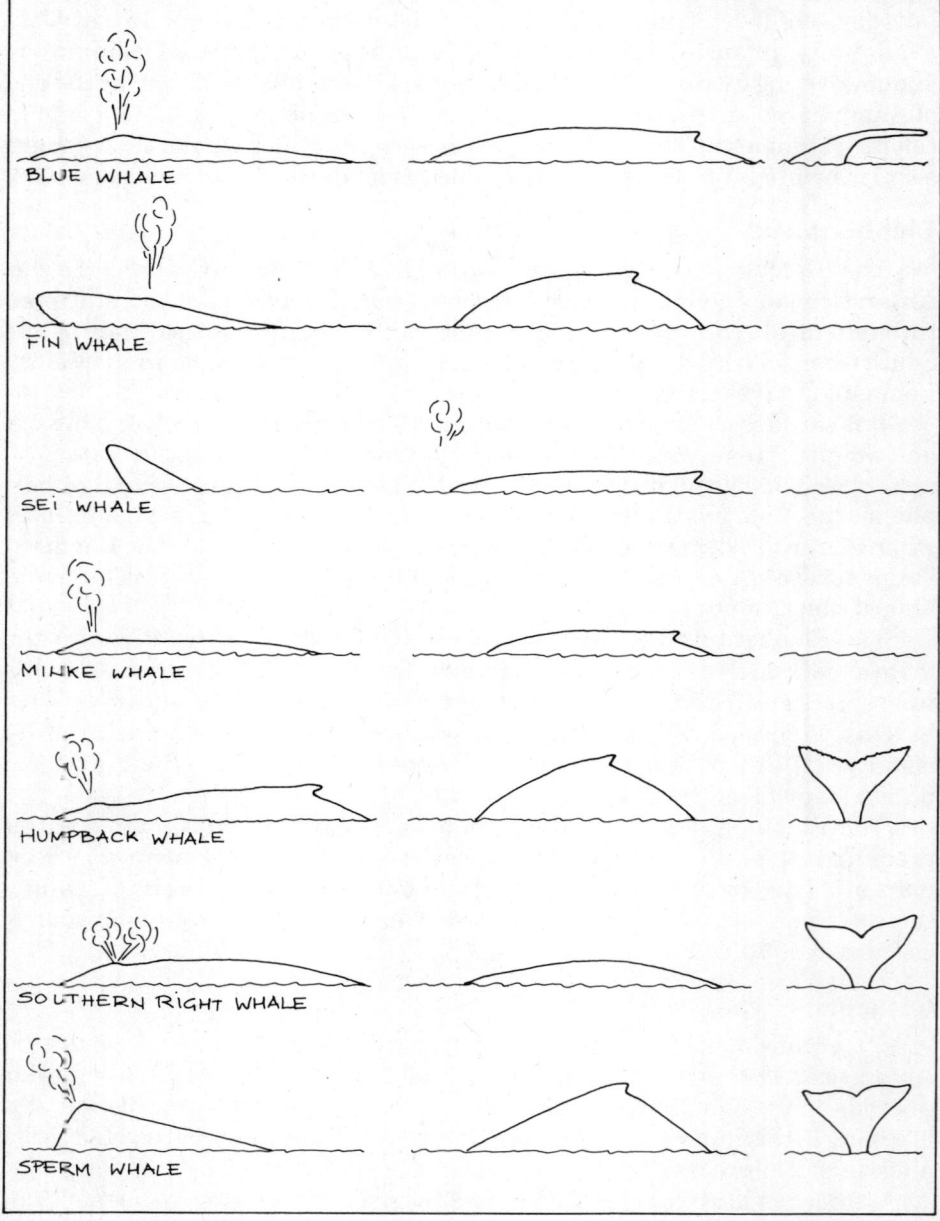

ment, although their ancestors were land animals. They are the largest living creatures, capable of reaching enormous sizes, as in the case of the Blue whale, which can exceed 25 meters in length and 100 tons in weight. They have a relatively thin skin with an underlying thick layer of fat, which ensures their thermal insulation and is a nutritional reserve in case of food shortage. In the process of aquatic specialization they have lost their rear limbs and have transformed their fore limbs into side flippers, still with bones. Not all cetaceans have a dorsal fin, the shape and dimension of which varies according to species. Their tail fin acts as a propellor and, unlike the tail fin of a fish, is horizontal to the body.

According to their dentition cetaceans may be subdivided into two large sub-orders: the toothed whales, or Odontoceti, and the baleen whales, or Mysticeti. The first group includes whales with a strong and non-differentiated set of teeth varying in number from 2 to 260; in the second group, teeth are replaced by baleen plates, fringed horny formations which hang from the palate and work as filters to retain the small organisms, mostly krill, on which the whales feed.

In spite of their perfect adaptation to the marine environment, cetaceans have to come to the surface to breathe and inhale air through the blowhole or spiracle situated on the top of their head. They can remain under water for varying periods of time, up to 60 minutes or more for certain species; the depth of the dive varies according to the size and nutritional habits of each whale and, in some cases, can reach several hundred meters. When whales re-emerge they expel both the air contained in the lungs and the condensation which has formed in the upper respiratory tract; this combined effect produces the well-known water spout, the shape, size and direction of which is peculiar to each species.

In order to reproduce whales abandon the cold Antarctic waters in search of more temperate and protected seas. The coupling process is the same as for any other mammal and, after a gestation period varying from 10 to 16 months, the female gives birth every 2 or 3 years to one calf. Unlike other mammals, the calf is born tail fin first in order to avoid drowning during delivery and is then taken immediately to the surface to breathe. The new-born calf can measure up to 1/3 of the size of its mother, who suckles it for a variable period from 6 to 12 months according to species. Together with their mothers young whales then begin their first migration towards the south, where they can more easily find the food resources which will allow them to develop their as yet unformed layer of fat. Considering that their average life span may in some cases exceed 100 years, cetaceans become sexually mature relatively early, between the 3rd and 8th year of age, while the body is still developing.

The diet of whales and dolphins is extremely varied as during their annual migrations they feed on local resources. During the reproduction period they live on their fat reserve, while in summer when they migrate back to Antarctica their food consumption increases substantially. Baleen whales feed on crustaceans, squid and fish, but many of them feed almost exclusively on krill, which they ingest in huge quantities. Toothed whales also feed on warm-blooded prey and the Killer whale in particular feeds on penguins, seals and occasionally baleen whales.

Cetaceans are generally not solitary animals and often gather in small groups known as schools, which in some periods of the year can increase in number. Large schools are often led by an adult male. Whales appear to display co-operative social behavior, in particular to obtain food, to aid coupling and delivery, and to protect young or injured animals.

They basically emit two kinds of sounds, one of which is used to locate obstacles and food, and the other to communicate. They do not have vocal cords, but have instead a series of nasal sacs under the spiracle, with the passage of air from one sac to the other creating their distinctive sounds. They also jump out of the sea and beat their tail fin and side flippers, causing water displacements which appear to be used as a means of communication.

More than a dozen different species of cetacean usually come each year to Antarctica. Among the best-known baleen whales are:

Blue whale

BLUE WHALE (*Balaenoptera musculus*): largest existing mammal, over 25 meters in length and 100 tons in weight; grey-blue skin color; about 100 skin folds covering its abdomen; small curved dorsal fin situated on the rear back; mouth equipped with approximately 640 baleen plates; gestation of 11-12 months and birth of one calf every 2 years; lactation period of 7 months; sexual maturity at 4-7 years of age; average life span of 80 years; diet predominantly based on krill; dive span from 10 to 20 minutes; strong and vertical water spout 6-12 meters high; solitary habits; summer circulation in circumpolar waters; southern hemisphere stock estimated at 5,000-6,000.

Fin whale

FIN WHALE (*Balaenoptera physalus*): over 20 meters in length and 50 tons in weight; very dark back and white abdomen covered by 50-60 skin folds; rear dorsal fin about 60 cm high; mouth equipped with 600-800 baleen plates; gestation of 12 months and birth of one calf every 2 years; lactation period of 6 months; sexual maturity at 5-8 years of age; life span close to 100 years; diet based on fish and plankton; dive span from 20 to 50 minutes; vertical water spout 4-6 meters high; schools of 20-100 individuals; summer circulation in circumpolar waters; southern stock estimated at approximately 70,000.

Sei whale

SEI WHALE (*Balaenoptera borealis*): similar to the Fin whale but a little smaller; dark blue back and white abdomen with 50 skin folds; mouth equipped with about 700 baleen plates; sharpened dorsal fin in the middle of the back; gestation of 12 months and birth of one calf every 2-3 years; lactation period of 6 months; sexual maturity at 7-9 years of age; average life span of 70 years; diet based on small crustaceans, predominantly krill; fast swimmer; conical water spout about 3 meters high; summer circulation between latitudes 30° S and 60° S; southern stock estimated at 50,000-100,000.

Minke whale

MINKE WHALE (*Balaenoptera acutorostrata*): measures about 8 meters and weighs approximately 7 tons; tapering body; very dark back, white abdomen with 60-70 skin folds and white strips over the side flippers; mouth equipped with 650 baleen plates; curved dorsal fin; gestation of 10-11 months; lactation period of 6 months; average life span of 50 years; diet based on plankton and squid; dive span up to 20 minutes; rarely visible water spout; summer circulation in circumpolar waters; world stock estimated between 150,000-300,000.

Humpback whale

HUMPBACK WHALE (*Balaenoptera novaeangliae*): massive body thinning towards the tail fin; about 15 meters in length and 30-40 tons in weight; humped back of very dark color; white abdomen with deep skin folds; small dorsal fin and long side flippers white in the lower part; mouth equipped with 600-700 baleen plates; gestation and lactation periods of almost 12 months; sexual maturity around 10 years of age; average life span of 50 years; diet based almost exclusively on krill; often jumps out of the water; dive span of almost 30 minutes; spheric water spout 3 meters high; summer circulation in circumpolar waters; southern stock estimated at 2,000-3,000.

Southern right whale

SOUTHERN RIGHT WHALE (*Eubalaena autralis*): about 15 meters in length and 50 tons in weight; dark grey body with clearer spots on the abdomen; numerous callouses of parasitic origin on the head; no dorsal fin; mouth with approximately 500 baleen plates; gestation period of 9-10 months; calf remains with the mother until 3rd year of age; sexual maturity around 10 years of age; average life span of 50 years; diet based on plankton and small crustaceans; slow swimmer; dive span of 10-20 minutes occasionally reaching 1 hour; double water spout 5 meters high with typical "V" shape; summer circulation south of latitude 40° S; southern stock estimated at 2,000-3,000.

Notable among the toothed whales visiting Antarctic waters are:

Sperm whale

SPERM WHALE (*Physeter catodon*): about 15 meters in length and 25-40 tons in weight; dark grey body; no dorsal fin and no abdominal skin folds; large head with trunked snout accounting for almost 1/3 of the body length; head with a cavity containing spermaceti, or sperm-oil; mouth located in the lower part of the head equipped with 20-26 teeth in the lower jaw; gestation of 16 months and birth of one calf every 3 years; 12 month lactation period; average life span of 60 years; sexual maturity around 10 years of age; formation of harems and of family groups of 20-50 whales; diet based mostly on giant squid, but also crustaceans and fish; deep dive and dive span exceeding 60 minutes; slanting water spout up to 5 meters high; summer circulation in subpolar waters; southern stock estimated at about 380,000.

Killer whale

KILLER WHALE (*Orcinus orca*): 7-8 meters in length and 5-8 tons in weight; black back, white from the lower jaw to the abdomen and over the eyes; triangular dorsal fin up to 2 meters high; conical head and mouth equipped with 20-28 well-developed teeth; gestation of 12-14 months and calf dependency of 1 year; schools of 8-15 whales and isolated couples; diet based on crustaceans, fish and squid, as well as penguins, seals, dolphins and baleen whales; circulation in circumpolar waters.

Birds

Among the varied seabirds inhabiting Antarctica, penguins are perhaps the best-known, often taken as a symbol for the local fauna. They are the most numerous species and represent about 90% of all birds in Antarctica, estimated at about 100 million.

Penguins

Of the 17-18 different species of penguin worldwide less than half inhabit the circumpolar region. The three species of the genus *Pygoscelis*, the Adélie, Gentoo and Chinstrap penguins live both in Antarctic and subantarctic areas. The Emperor penguin is probably the most representative of all Antarctic inhabitants as it never abandons the iced continent, while the King penguin has a more subpolar distribution and may only occasionally be seen along the Antarctic coast. Another two species of the genus *Eudyptes*, the Macaroni and Rockhopper penguins, live in circumpolar cool temperate regions and only exceptionally reach high latitudes.

The most striking feature of penguins is that they are flightless birds which have adapted totally to their marine environment, though they have not abandoned the land where they complete reproduction and moulting cycles. It is interesting to note, however, that penguins have maintained their ability to fly in the water; their aquatic propulsion is the result of wing movement which in effect simulates aerial flight, and their webbed feed perform the function only of a rudder.

A detailed study has been made of the genetic origins and past physiology of penguins on the basis of fossils found in different areas of the southern hemisphere. It appears that their ancestors were flying birds which evolved losing aerial flight capacity in order to adapt to new environmental conditions, probably as a result of changes in food availability. Comparative studies have also been undertaken on recently extinct birds such as the Great auk, which also lost aerial flight but maintained aquatic flight, as well as on other species

Pygoscelis penguins

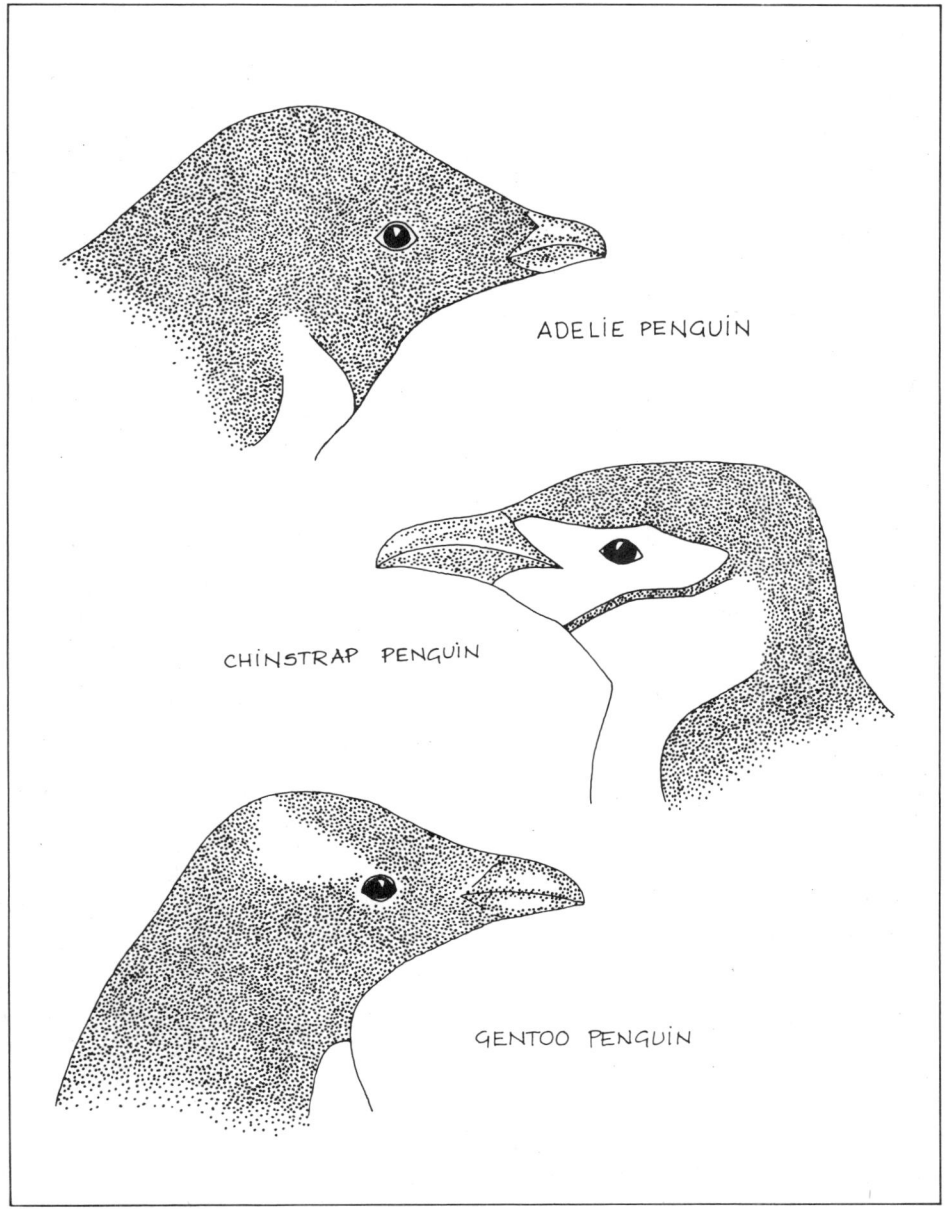

ADELIE PENGUIN

CHINSTRAP PENGUIN

GENTOO PENGUIN

of living birds such as the Diving petrel, capable of both aerial and aquatic flight.

The evolution of penguins represents a complete and sophisticated adaptation to the marine environment, in particular for the Antarctic species, settled in the coldest and most inhospitable region on earth. Penguins are warm-blooded animals with a body temperature of 37°/38°C and have adapted thermally at different levels, both to retain and reduce body heat. First, it may be observed that larger-size penguins, such as the Emperor, live in the coldest part of Antarctica. This appears to be related to the fact that heat generation depends on body volume and thus a larger body loses relatively less heat than a smaller one. Next, the body of the penguin has an underlying thick layer of fat representing up to 1/3 of its weight, which has the double function of thermal insulation and of an energy reserve in case of forced fasts during breeding or moulting. Finally, their skin is completely covered with feathers overlapping each other like scales and forming a surface totally impermeable to water and wind.

Penguins are so well-insulated that they may occasionally need to reduce their body heat, which they do by ruffling their feathers and thus exposing their skin to the cold air. Overheating appears to be the main reason why penguins do not cross the equatorial region into the northern hemisphere.

Penguins are well-known for their clumsiness on land, obliged by their body shape to carry their weight on the back of their feet. They walk counterbalancing their movements with their open wings, with each step seemingly a difficult struggle to maintain balance; if possible they slide downhill on their stomach.

Contrasting surprisingly with this clumsiness on land is their perfect aquatic adaptation. At sea their body acquires a hydrodynamic shape and literally flies in the water, propelled by its wings acting as flippers. When swimming, penguins often jump out of the water for some distance, drop back and regain their speed, which can reach as much as 30 km/h. This is to enable breathing as they cannot dive for long periods; the duration and depth of the dive varies according to species, with average dives rarely exceeding 3 minutes.

Their diet is based almost exclusively on crustaceans, squid and fish, although the Antarctic species also feed on krill. Like all seabirds, penguins have a special secretion mechanism which eliminates excess salt contained in food and seawater; two special glands located at the base of the nasal cavities extract the salty solution from the blood and expel it through the penguin's breathing openings.

Adélies, Gentoos and Chinstraps

The most common Antarctic penguins are the Adélie, Gentoo and Chinstrap species, of the genus *Pygoscelis*. The Adélie penguin (*P. adeliae*) is black, including the head and bill, with a white front; the Gentoo penguin (*P. papua*) is also black on its back and white on its front and is easily recognizable by its red bill and the white band on the top of its head between the eyes; the third species, the Chinstrap penguin (*P. antarctica*) is very similar to the Adélie, but the area around the eyes, chin and cheeks is white and a thin black strip crosses its chin.

All three species are very similar in size with an average height of 60-70 cm and an average weight of 4.5-6 kg, with Gentoos a little bigger. It is not unusual to find penguins of much less than average weight; this is generally the result of the forced fast periods they undergo during incubation and moulting.

The breeding range of *Pygoscelis* penguins covers a wide area within the Antarctic Convergence, from the continental coast up to the subantarctic islands. They all have colonial habits and nest in rookeries which can comprise thousands of birds. As they inhabit the same environment, breeding areas may be common to the three species, which also display very similar reproduction patterns.

They spend most of the winter dispersed in the ocean close to the pack ice limit, and only at the beginning of October do they migrate to ice-free coastal areas; guided by instinct they almost always return to the same place where they were born or bred in the past year. The males usually arrive first and, after defining their territory, begin to build their nests. Nests are circular, about 30-40 cm in diameter, and are built with pebbles and other solid material.

A short time later the females arrive and couple formation begins. Formerly mated males and females usually mate again even though they have spent the whole winter separately, recognizing each other through sounds and cries. Couples are formed after a period of courtship and ritual behavior during which the penguins remain ashore and fast. The settlement of a colony is usually accompanied by vociferous clamor and frequent quarrels until nest building is over, and in late October the female lays two eggs. She immediately returns to sea to feed herself and leaves her companion in charge of incubating the eggs. Periodically one parent relieves the other, with releases becoming increasingly shorter until the chicks are born at around 36 days.

New-born penguins are covered with a very soft dark fluff and nestle for about two weeks under one of the parents until they have grown larger and replaced their fluff with a coarser brown down. During the entire breeding period they depend exclusively on their parents for food, regurgitated into their mouths by the parent on duty at sea. They are extremely greedy and can devour the equivalent of their weight in food in a few minutes.

As the chicks grow older and become more independent they often gather in groups called *crèches* while adults go to sea to feed. The *crèche* acts as a sort of nursery with a protective function for retaining body heat and reducing predatory attacks by seabirds, especially the skua which is the penguin's principal enemy.

Only in late summer do the chicks replace their fluff with a full but immature plumage, impermeable to water and wind. This is a major event in the penguin life cycle as it allows juveniles to enter the sea safely for the first time and thus to become self-sufficient for feeding. A short time later the adults also undergo their annual moulting and are obliged to stay out of the sea and fast for 2-3 weeks, until they acquire a new plumage and can begin their winter migration. Juveniles acquire adult plumage only in their second year and usually become sexually mature at around the fifth year.

Emperors

The Emperor penguin (*Aptenodytes forsteri*) is the largest of all penguins, with an average height of 100-120 cm and a weight of 30 kg, varying consistently from 20 kg up to 40 kg because of the severe fast it undergoes during reproduction. Its back is a dark blue-grey and its front is white, while its head is black with two distinctive yellow patches on both sides which join in the upper part of the breast. The bill is pronounced and curved downwards and its feet are almost completely covered by the lower part of the abdomen.

The Emperor penguin is considered the only "true" Antarctic penguin as it inhabits the most remote latitudes and, unlike other species, does not migrate towards subantarctic regions. Its life cycle is characterized by two particular aspects, which make it the most outstanding example of environmental adaptation.

First, it inhabits areas permanently covered by ice and does not have any contact with ice-free ground. This means that it cannot build any kind of nest and is obliged to hold the egg it lays on its feet, sheltering it beneath the low abdominal fold specially equipped for this purpose with a thick layer of fat. This explains why it can lay only one egg.

Second, its seasonal rhythm is totally out of phase with that of other penguins as it spends summer at sea and begins its reproduction cycle in winter under the most adverse climatic conditions. This seemingly incomprehensible behavior is explained by the fact that in order to survive, the chick must replace its fluff with juvenile waterproof plumage during summer in order to have enough time to feed and grow before the coming winter.

The Emperor penguin has colonial habits and at the beginning of autumn usually begins gathering in rookeries in which, unlike other penguins, it does not define a territory. Courtship and couple formation takes place following ritual behavior. The female's egg is laid in early May and is taken over by the male who shelters it on its feet beneath the abdomen, while females leave together for the sea in search of food.

For the two months necessary for incubation the males remain together in the same place until the females come back to release them. They stay on an absolute fast for an overall period of about 3 months and live on the fat supplies accumulated during summer which also provide thermal protection. In order to defend themselves from winter temperatures and icy blizzards, males display social behavior and group together in a so-called *tortue*, a formation of individuals standing as closely as possible to each other.

The female usually returns at about the time hatching takes place and searches with loud sounds and cries in the crowded rookery for its mate, with which it has lost all contact. The starving males then march together towards the ice-free sea which at that time of year may be several thousand kilometers away, while the female begins feeding its chick with the food stored and brought back.

The new-born Emperor is covered with a soft fluff of a light grey color turning darker on the head, except for a wide white patch surrounding each eye. Breeding behavior similar to that of other penguins can also be observed among Emperors. As spring comes closer and the pack ice begins to break up, parents release each other more frequently and have more chance to feed themselves. In early summer the chick starts moulting and acquires its first impermeable plumage and is finally capable of diving into the sea and becoming self-sufficient in feeding. The chick may eventually complete its moult on ice floes, but before the end of summer it must have had enough time to grow and to attain a body size large enough to survive the next Antarctic winter.

Kings

The King penguin (*Aptenodytes patagonicus*) is very similar to the Emperor, but weighs about half as much and measures about 20 cm less. Its color is very much the same except for the ear patch which is orange rather than yellow; the bill is more pronounced, and the feet are free from the abdominal fold.

Although these two species of penguin belong to the same genus and are very similar, they live in entirely different areas. The King penguin breeds in the subantarctic islands north of the pack ice limit, almost at the edge of the Antarctic Convergence, and gathers in crowded rookeries situated in low areas close to the shore. Although it lives on ice-free ground, like the Emperor it does not build a nest and lays only one egg, which is incubated on its feet.

After courtship and couple formation the King penguin lays its egg almost any time between November and March, but with two peak periods, one at the beginning and the other at the end of summer. The egg is incubated for a little less than two months and breeding behavior is very much the same as for all penguins, with the advantage that the parents can release each other quite often.

The young chick is covered with a uniform dark brown fluff and is fed by its parents by regurgitation. Unlike other chicks, it spends all winter at the colony and only in the following spring is its fluff is replaced by the juvenile waterproof plumage which enables it to become independent. The parents then moult, court and can again begin the reproduction cycle.

The most surprising feature of the King penguin's life cycle is that it does not follow an annual pattern, as the time span between each egg laying varies from 14 to 16 months. This means that an early summer breeder may the following year be a late summer breeder, but it is then unlikely that the following year the female will succeed in breeding in winter months.

Macaronis and Rockhoppers

The Macaroni (*Eudyptes crysolophus*) and Rockhopper (*Eudyptes cres-*

tatus) penguins look very much like the Adélie but with a very distinctive yellow feather tuft on both sides of the head. The Macaroni is about the same size as the Adélie (about 4.5 kg) while the Rockhopper is a little smaller (about 2.5 kg).

The breeding range of crested penguins covers the subantarctic area, in particular cool temperate islands, and Macaronis occasionally nest as far south as the Antarctic Peninsula. They have colonial habits and form very crowded rookeries, where they breed every year. They follow the reproduction and breeding pattern of most penguins and lay two eggs in early spring. Both parents incubate the eggs in the nest for about 5 weeks, but tend to discard or lose the first, usually smaller than the second, and breed only one chick.

Young crested penguins grow relatively fast and after about 10 weeks moult and acquire waterproof plumage, becoming independent from their parents.

Seabirds

More than 30 different species of seabird annually visit the coasts of Antarctica and the subantarctic islands. Their migration towards southern latitudes is seasonal and their distribution is scattered in the circumpolar area according to pack ice movement and thus to availability of food.

They usually arrive in Antarctica in late spring when the marine ice begins to break up. Most seabirds nest in the region and spend all summer breeding their chicks and feeding on the abundant resources of the Antarctic Ocean. Their diet is based mostly on plankton, crustaceans, squid and fish. When winter approaches and the sea starts to freeze, they migrate north again towards more temperate areas.

Albatross

The albatross (*Diomedeidae* family) is probably the most attractive of all Antarctic seabirds for its majestic style of flight. Amongst the largest existing birds with a wing span ranging from 200 cm to 350 cm, its body is usually white and the upper part of its wings black, although this can vary according to species and age. Its beak is long and strong and has an independent nasal passage on both sides. Its large wings allow it to glide in the air and to fly over extremely long distances with a minimum energy consumption.

The albatross has well-defined marine habits and stays on land only to reproduce. It occasionally nests in small colonies and lays one egg every two years which is incubated for a variable time span of 60-90 days. The chick is fed by the parents by regurgitation and its dependency lasts almost 7 months.

Several species of albatross are found in Antarctica, among them the Wandering albatross, the Royal albatross, the Black-browed albatross and the Light-mantled sooty albatross.

Petrels and fulmars

The family of *Procellariidae* includes several species of petrels and fulmars. Their shape is very much the same as that of the albatross, although they are somewhat smaller and have only one nasal passage on the top of the beak separated by a thin inside wall. Their coloring varies according to species. Like the albatross they have a gliding flight style but their smaller wing span, varying from 80 cm to 220 cm, causes them to use more frequent wing movements. They stay on land to breed and occasionally nest in colonies; eggs are incubated for 30-60 days and chicks are able to fly after about two months.

The largest of all antarctic petrels is the Southern giant petrel, of dark brown color, although some albino specimens can also be found. Among smaller petrels, the Cape petrel is easily recognizable by its spotted black and white coloring and its habit of nesting on steep cliffs. The silver-grey Antarctic fulmar may often be seen flying over polar waters with its typical semicircular glide. Other species of *Procellariidae* which may frequently be seen are the Grey and the Antarctic petrels, as well as several species of prion.

The small storm petrel (family *Hydrobatidae*) can be recognized by the continuous wing movement due to its reduced wing span of about 40 cm; the most common is the Wilson storm petrel, black with a white strip over the tail, which usually builds its nests in small holes in stony areas.

Cormorant

Another typical inhabitant of the Antarctic coast is the Blue-eyed cormorant (family *Phalacrocoracidae*), or Imperial shag. All black with white neck and breast, it is distinguishable by its blue eyes and the small tuft that appears on its head during the reproduction period; it has a pronounced beak with a yellow caruncle, a small fleshy protuberance, on its base. It is specialized in diving to obtain its food. It has colonial habits and lays 2-3 eggs in crater-like nests built with guano, kelp and solid material.

Skua

Of all Antarctic seabirds the Skua (family *Stercoraridae*) is notable for its predator activity around the colonies of other birds, especially penguins. It is a dark brown gull-like bird with white-tipped wings. It scavenges and will fly over penguin rookeries in search of eggs or young chicks momentarily left unprotected by their parents.

Snowy sheatbill

The Snowy sheatbill (family *Chionididae*) is a completely white bird resembling a large pigeon and has habits similar to those of the Skua. It is not a good flyer and is well-known for its ability to walk for relatively long distances in coastal areas.

Southern gull

The Southern gull (family *Laridae*) is a coastal bird which feeds on almost anything edible. Its body is white with the upper part of its wings black; it has a yellow beak and feet. It is a good flyer but very rarely dives into the sea.

Antarctic tern

The Antarctic tern (family *Laridae*) is a small elegant bird of light grey color with a red beak and feet and a black hood on the top of its head. Its wings are long and slim and its flight style is characterized by frequent wing movements and vertical dives into the sea. It is very tenacious and defends its nest even against larger aggressors, attacking them with its sharp beak.

CHAPTER **6**

History of discoveries and conquests

Premise

Antarctica is a word of Greek origin comprising the words *anti* (opposite) and *arktos* (bear), the latter referring to the polar star of the Ursa Minor constellation, or Little Bear. This etymological origin suggests that, on the basis of the Theory of Opposites or Symmetries, the Greeks supposed the existence of an Unknown Land opposite their own. It subsequently took over two millennia, through centuries which often saw the persecution of science, to demonstrate that the earth was round and to confirm the existence of the legendary continent opposite the Arctic.

This time lapse had a major influence on the Antarctic pattern of exploration and expansion, absolutely unique if compared to that in any other land. Antarctica in effect is not only the last continent to have been discovered by man, but its actual conquest is very recent, with human expansion concentrated into a very short time span. Antarctica moreover was not inhabited by any native population and this exceptional condition excluded the view of expansion in terms of assertion of cultural, political or economic supremacy over another culture; it played an important role in facilitating the simultaneous participation of several nations in the management of the continent, without the exclusive leadership of one country.

Historical stages

The early exploration of Antarctica began with a "conceptual" phase characterized by exploration aimed at demonstrating the real existence of the famous Unknown Land. Courageous explorers essentially took on the unknown, some of them succeeding in discovering new southern lands occasionally helped by chance events. Once the sixth continent had been located its easily accessible resources allowed intensive exploitation by sealers and whalers, who became the first true Antarctic explorers and contributed substantially to the survey of the local coastal topography.

At about the same time the new continent began to attract the attention of the international scientific community. Expeditions became progressively more scientific in nature, aided by the rapid technological progress brought about by the industrial revolution.

The final phase came with the settlement of man on the continent. Expansion, though carried out in the name of scientific research, was also

Area of early Antarctic exploration

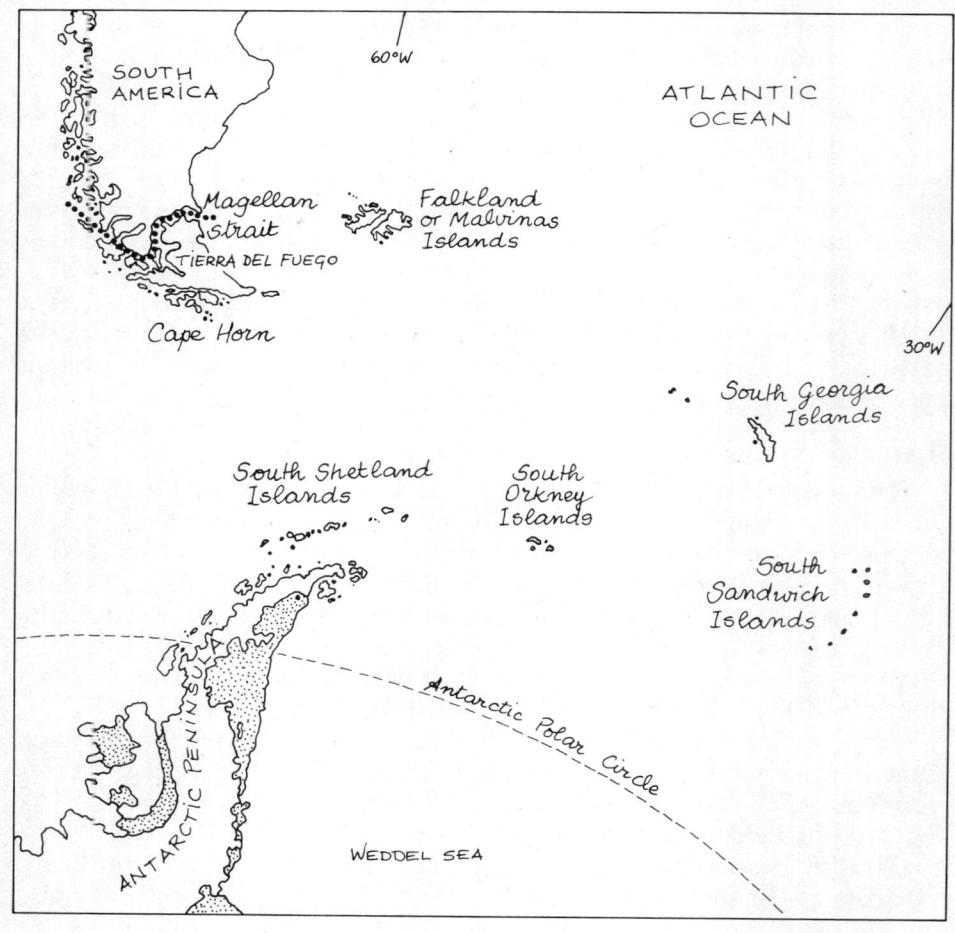

combined with nationalist claims and new prospects for economic exploitation. Only in 1959, with the signing of the Antarctic Treaty and the acceptance of the revolutionary view of shared management of the continent, did the international community enter the modern phase of Antarctic history.

Magellan, 1520

After the Greeks' supposition of the "opposite" land, the turning point in Antarctic history was Magellan's discovery in 1520 of the strait which today carries his name. Under the patronage of the Spanish Crown, the Portuguese explorer was searching for the eastern passage to the Indies and thought that the land south of the strait, the Land of the Fires (Tierra del Fuego), was the northern limit of the Unknown Continent.

On the basis of this discovery the outline of a new continent called Terra Australis Incognita (Unknown Southern Land), occupying the whole area from south of the Magellan Strait up to the pole, appeared on the first maps of the time.

Hoces and Drake 1526 and, 1578

This vision of the southern hemisphere was maintained for most of the 16th century, until the first doubts were raised following the chance deviation south of some explorer ships attempting to sail through the strait. In 1526 and in 1578, the Spanish explorer Fernando Hoces and Sir Francis Drake respectively reported what they described as the end of all lands where the Atlantic and Pacific Oceans met in one large ocean.

Schouten and Le Maire, 1616

In 1616 a Dutch expedition under the command of Schooten and Le Maire succeeded in discovering Cape Horn, putting an end to the argument of whether Tierra del Fuego was part of the Unknown Continent.

1700s

The end of the 17th and most of the 18th centuries saw several voyages of exploration to the Cape Horn area and towards new eastern territories. It was during this period that the Kerguelen Islands and the South Georgia Islands, first called the San Pedro Islands, were discovered.

Cook, 1770-75

Following these sporadic expeditions, the voyage around the world of James Cook between 1770 and 1775 may be considered the first with a general scientific purpose. In the service of the Royal Society of Science, Cook left England charged with exploring and circumnavigating the Unknown Continent.

In command of the *Endeavour*, he made a first voyage around New Zealand until then believed, with Australia, to be part of the Unknown Continent. In his second voyage on board the *Resolution* and the *Adventure*, Cook circumnavigated the earth at latitudes never before explored and sailed as far south as 71° S. He crossed the Antarctic Polar Circle three times and sailed along the line of the pack ice, but without sighting the legendary continent.

He confirmed the discovery of the South Georgia Islands and re-named them in honor of King George I; he also discovered a territory which he was not able to define as continental or insular, naming it the Land of Sandwich. Cook finally returned to England after a voyage of 3 years and over 6,000 miles, convinced that the Unknown Land did not exist.

1800s

As the end of the century approached, the international political balance was altered by important changes which had repercussions on the pattern of expansion of several nations.

West of the Atlantic, the first signs of political and economic independence from Spain started to show in most South American countries, while the United States was undergoing a phase of rapid growth after independence in 1776. In Europe, after the decline of the Napoleonic era, Great Britain asserted its political supremacy through a clear expansion policy and the Russian Empire attained its peak of prosperity under Czar Alexander I.

The immediate consequence of this phase of world expansion was a growing interest in new territories in which new resources could be found. Special attention was focused on the southern regions, especially as early explorers reported the existence of large seal and sea lion stocks.

Sealers

The early 19th century saw the progressive growth of sealing in the southern seas, expanding from the Falklands or Malvinas to the South Georgia Islands, and then to the Antarctic Peninsula. In a very short time it changed from a pioneer activity into a large-scale and extensive industry involving several nations, among them the United States, Great Britain and Argentina. Primary targets were the Elephant and Fur seal, for the exploitation of their fur and, in particular, of their fat from which oil was extracted and used in lighting.

Initially, sealers hunted individually; competition among them was so fierce that they were constantly in search of previously unexplored exploitable sites. In this way they became the first explorers of the insular area close to the Antarctic Peninsula, but it is extremely difficult to determine what lands were discovered first and by whom.

Smith, 1818

It appears that in 1818 Smith, a British trader en route to Valparaiso, was blown south of Cape Horn by a storm and sighted land, which would later come to be known as the South Shetland Islands, in which South American sealers had apparently already been operating for several years.

Palmer and Powell

In the same year, an American sealer, Palmer, while following a sealing ship, arrived at Deception Island (South Shetlands) where seal exploitation was apparently already established; Palmer, however, is held to be the first captain to have explored the South Shetland Islands and parts of the Antarctic Peninsula. In search of new exploitable areas he later decided to sail east together with a British sealer named Powell, and reached a previously unknown group of islands, which would later be called the South Orkneys.

Bellinghausen, 1819-21

In this period, primarily dominated by sealing, two Russian ships, the *Vostock* and the *Mirny*, approached Antarctic waters with totally different aims. Under the command of Thaddeus Bellinghausen, their task was to circumnavigate the still-unknown continent south of the latitudes explored by Cook. Bellinghausen succeeded in crossing the Antarctic Polar Circle on several occasions and explored the sea which today bears his name. He sighted what he thought to be continental land, naming it in honor of Alexander I, though it would later be found to be a large island on the western side of the Antarctic Peninsula. He also reached the South Shetland Islands, but discovered that his expedition had been preceded by sealers.

After the early stage of individual sealing, important trading and shipowning companies, among them Enderby Brothers of London, showed an increasing interest in seal exploitation and pressed for more specialization. In order to identify sealing sites more precisely, expeditions were charged with the drawing up of charts of the new lands.

Weddell, 1820-24

In this context, the British captain James Weddell spent four years from 1820 to 1824 in the South Shetland area, hunting and exploring. In 1823 he decided to chart the sea south of the South Orkney Islands and, with very favorable pack ice conditions, succeeded in sailing up to latitude 74°15' S into the sea which today carries his name.

Foster, 1828-29

A few years later (1828-29), Captain Henry Foster, on a mission for the British Royal Society, explored the Antarctic Peninsula area and carried out the first meteorological and hydrographical surveys.

Biscoe, 1830-32

A new circumnavigation voyage was undertaken between 1830 and 1832 by John Biscoe who, while sealing, explored the northern coast of the Antarctic Peninsula which he named Graham Land.

Early scientific voyages

Reports of the discoveries made in these southern regions eventually reached the international scientific community, which began to show a growing interest in the Antarctic lands, especially after the publication by Gauss of important studies on earth magnetism in 1833. An important role was also played by the growing weight of national Royal Societies which highlighted the need to carry out exploration of still unknown regions following a more scientific approach. In the next few years, France, the United States and Great Britain decided to promote new missions aimed at exploring other areas of the new continent and searching for the magnetic South Pole.

D'Urville 1837-40

The first to sail from Europe in 1837, under the patronage of the Academy of Science of Paris, was Dumont D'Urville with the *Astrolabe* and the *Zelée*. The task of the Frenchman was to penetrate into the Antarctic sea at a more southerly latitude than Weddell and to make observations about earth physics. In his three year voyage, D'Urville explored the Antarctic Peninsula area and then sailed west through the Pacific Ocean. In 1840 he again headed south and finally sighted a continental land which he named after his wife Adélie.

Wilkes 1838-41

One year after D'Urville's departure, a large mission comprising six ships under the command of Lieutenant Charles Wilkes left the United States for Antarctica. After several misfortunes and the loss of part of the fleet, Wilkes' expedition ran into dense pack ice and only at the end of his voyage did he succeed in sailing along the Antarctic coast south of Australia.

Ross. 1839-43

At almost the same time the British Admiralty decided to send an expedition to Antarctica, with the aim of carrying out geographical, ocean-ographical and meteorological surveys, as well as making observations about magnetism, geology, botany and zoology. The mission was led by James Ross, who had recently discovered the magnetic North Pole. Ross left England in 1839 with the *Erebus* and the *Terror*; he sailed through the Cape of Good Hope, passed Tasmania and reached the Antarctic continent in the area which he named Cape Andare. He continued sailing south, but was stopped at latitude 78°04' S by a huge barrier of ice which would later be called the Ross Ice Shelf. He charted the region and detected some continental mountain chains and volcanos, naming them after his ships. Later, Ross moved towards the Antarctic Peninsula and attempted to sail through the Weddell Sea, but was obstructed by pack ice.

The following years saw a period of inactivity in Antarctic exploration, due to new political events which dominated the international scene. Several nations were experiencing periods of internal political instability and concentrated their attention on home affairs. From 1861 to 1865 the United States was torn by the Civil War and in the decades 1850-70 several European nations went through delicate unification processes, while France was facing war with the Prussian Empire.

Steam navigation

This period also coincided with the end of a historical phase in exploration, as traditional sailing techniques were completely overturned by technological innovations brought about by the industrial revolution. The invention of the steam engine and the propeller saw the advent of steam navigation, affecting the prospects for major expansion.

Whalers

These revolutionary innovations were very soon incorporated into most sectors of the nautical world. They were also adopted by whalers who, throughout the century, had been hunting extensively in the cold seas of the northern hemisphere. As a result of the combined effects of steam navigation and the invention by the Norwegians of the harpoon gun, whale exploitation increased greatly; in a few years, the northern whale population was so depleted that whalers began expanding towards the southern hemisphere, where stocks were virtually untouched. In the final decades of the 1800s, the first whaling ships appeared in the Antarctic Ocean prospecting for the best exploitable areas and, in a very short time, pioneer whaling reached an industrial scale, turning into one of the most competitive and exhaustive economic exploitations ever undertaken by man.

Like sealers, whalers also contributed to the survey of the Antarctic topography. One of the first whaling companies to explore the Antarctic waters was that founded in Buenos Aires in 1892 by the Norwegian sailor Carl Larsen, who would later take part in a Swedish scientific expedition to Antarctica. Other whaling companies appeared shortly after, such as the Magellan Whaling Co. of Punta Arenas, Chile and the Hecktor Whaling Co. of Norwegian origin, both of which operated off Deception Island in the South Shetlands. The first permanent whaling station was opened in 1904 in Grytviken in the South Georgia Islands.

Towards the end of the 19th century the technological progress brought about by the industrial revolution had a major impact on world expansion patterns both in practical and theoretical terms. New means of transport allowed less dependency on natural agents and new inventions resulted in a general modernization of equipment; furthermore, the direct contribution of science in developing these new technologies highlighted its importance in the industrialization process taking place at that time. This new view of science as an applied discipline, fundamental to development projects, allowed the growing participation of the scientific community both in national and international affairs, at the same time establishing the foundation for closer international scientific co-operation which began to be apparent in several fields. This evolution also affected the approach to exploration of new regions of the globe, making it a systematic and well-defined discipline within the broader frame of geographical sciences.

1st International Polar Year, 1882-83

As far as Antarctica was concerned, interest in the white continent acquired an increasingly clear scientific character and the declaration of the 1st International Polar Year in 1882 represents the first attempt to call world attention to the need to build a basic geographical knowledge about these remote regions.

6th International Congress on Geography 1895

The first integrated project of a scientific nature, however, was proposed some time later during the 6th International Congress on Geography held in London in 1895. On that occasion it was expressly recommended that all scientific societies press their respective governments to promote the exploration of Antarctica and to sponsor exploratory missions with scientific objectives. This pressure can be interpreted as the first step towards a new phase in Antarctic exploration which would lead to the conquest of the South Pole, and would pass into history as the Antarctic heroic era. It was also the first example of the scientific co-operation which would culminate in the International Geophysical Year of 1957, considered to be the starting point of modern Antarctic science.

Gerlache

Between 1897 and 1899 two different expeditions eft Europe and headed south. The first was led by Adrien de Gerlache, a Belgian biologist, accompanied by a young Norwegian named Roald Amundsen who a short time later would become one of the best-known Antarctic explorers. Gerlache charted the western part of the Antarctic Peninsula and succeeded in identifying several groups of islands along the continental coast. At latitude 71° S his ship was trapped by pack ice and was forced to spend the winter in Antarctica.

Borchgrevink

The second expedition was led by Carsten Borchgrevink, whose aim was to spend a winter on the continent. He landed in the Cape Andare area, built a base camp and explored the neighboring region using skis and dogsledges hauled by huskies, following the Scandinavian tradition.

7th International Congress on Geography, 1899

For the next International Congress on Geography held in Berlin in 1899 the Antarctic question was still considered to be the main item on the agenda. Participants emphasized the inadequacy of isolated expeditions and pressed for the establishment of a co-operative project involving all nations interested in scientific research. The result of this renewed pressure by the Congress was the successful organization of the International Expedition to Antarctica, organized by Germany, Sweden, Great Britain and France, who sent five national missions between 1901 and 1905.

Drygalsky, 1901-04

The expedition organized by the German Admiralty (1901-04) was headed by Professor Von Drygalsky, who explored the Antarctic coast south of the Indian Ocean and landed in a continental area which he named in honor of Kaiser William II.

Nordenskjöld, 1901-04

The Swedish mission (1901-04) was led by Dr. Otto Nordenskjöld, an explorer well-known for his journeys in Patagonia; its ship, the *Antarctic*, was commanded by Carl Larsen, an experienced whaler. The aim of the expedition was to explore the Antarctic Peninsula and its neighboring islands, and to establish a winter camp in order to carry out meteorological and magnetic observation.

Nordenskjöld and five companions landed on Snow Hill Island, on which they planned to spend the winter. Larsen sailed back to Tierra del Fuego and the following year returned to Antarctica to pick up the group, but his ship was cut off by pack ice which crushed and sank it. The crew was able to find shelter on a small island, where a few men decided to leave the main party and make for the Snow Hill Camp. The three groups remained isolated from each other during the following winter and were finally rescued in 1903 by the Argentine corvette *Uruguay*.

Scott, 1901-04

At about the same time the British expedition (1901-04) led by Robert Scott left England on board the *Discovery*. Scott sailed into the Ross Sea and made a detailed exploration of the coast in the McMurdo Bay area; he also flew over the Ross Ice Shelf in a balloon. He landed on the continent and together with Ernest Shackleton marched towards the South for three months, but snowstorms and increasing difficulties forced him to turn back at latitude 82° S.

Bruce, 1902-04

As part of the British commitment to Antarctic research, a new expedition left Europe in 1902 on the *Scotia*, led by the Scotsman Dr. William Bruce. The mission headed towards the Weddell Sea, but was forced by dense pack ice to sail back to the South Orkney Islands where on Laurie Island Bruce established a small meteorological and magnetic station, called Osmond House. Aware that his expedition could not ensure continuity in observation in the future, Bruce offered the settlement to the Argentine government, who took it over in 1903. Osmond House became the first permanent Antarctic establishment and has functioned continuously since its foundation.

Charcot, 1903-05

The last mission to make up the International Antarctic Expedition was French, led by Charcot on board the *Français* (1903-05). Charcot met with Bruce and Nordenskjöld in Buenos Aires and then sailed for the Antarctic Peninsula, where he spent one year carrying out oceanographical, geographical and environmental surveys.

1908-10

Charcot repeated the voyage in 1908-10 with the *Pourquoi-pas*, a ship specially equipped for polar waters. He continued the exploration of the Peninsula and of other coastal areas, obtaining outstanding scientific results.

The heroic era

Charcot's expedition marked the conclusion of the phase opened by the Berlin Congress and the international community appeared satisfied with the results so far obtained. Many doubts still existed, however, about the inland area of Antarctica, completely unexplored except for Scott's unsuccessful expedition in 1902. In the years which followed the exploration of the continental region became an increasingly pressing objective and the conquest of the South Pole gradually developped from a theoretical into a concrete aim. This also implied important changes in exploration methods, until then dependant almost exclusively on marine know-how, as inland targets demanded the development of new technologies incorporating land-borne transport and skills.

Shackleton, 1907-09

In this context, Shackleton's expedition between 1907 and 1909 may be considered as the first real attempt to reach the South Pole. On board the *Nimrod,* Shackleton headed for the McMurdo Strait in the Ross Sea, where he established his base camp.

The first important result was attained in 1909 after a 4 month journey over 2,000 km by three members of his team who succeeded in reaching the Magnetic South Pole (72° 25' S and 155° 16' E). At roughly the same time Shackleton, with a team of four, set off for the Geographical South Pole on sledges hauled by Siberian ponies, but the animals were not able to stand the severe conditions and had to be slaughtered. The explorers continued on foot and, in spite of the freezing climate, succeeded in reaching the polar plateau; but in January 1909, a shortage of food and other growing difficulties forced Shackleton to turn back at latitude 88° 23' S, just 180 km from the Pole.

Amundsen and Scott, 1911-12

As Shackleton headed back, new expeditions to the South Pole were already being discussed in Europe. Unlike previous years, however, the policy of joint efforts in view of common objectives was progressively being dropped and the South Pole gradually turned into a target for personal and national competition. In this climate of challenge, two expeditions left Europe in 1910 and in their attainment of the longed-for goal, opened one of the most dramatic pages in Antarctic history.

The British Expedition to Antarctica under the command of Robert Falcon Scott sailed from England in June on board the *Terranova*. A few months later Roald Amundsen left Scandinavia on board the *Fram*, having abandoned his original plans for an expedition to the North Pole as Peary had successfully anticipated him a short time before.

The two expeditions arrived in Antarctica at the beginning of 1911 and settled in the Ross Sea Bay. Scott established his base camp on Ross Island and Amundsen on the opposite coast in Whale Bay, at a distance of just over 400 miles. They spent the first months planning their journeys and organizing food deposits, while waiting for their departure in the coming spring.

Amundsen set off for the South Pole at the beginning of September. One month later he reached the first deposit camp at latitude 80° S and left again with a team of only four, each man with a light sledge hauled by 13 dogs. The small group advanced inland, crossed several mountain chains and succeeded in reaching the polar highlands. In spite of the extremely severe conditions, they managed to cover an average distance of 25 km per day, their march made easier by their relatively light equipment and the fact that exhausted dogs were slaughtered in order to feed those remaining. Amundsen and his companions finally reached the South Pole on 14th December, 1911 and returned successfully to their base camp on January 25th after an uninterrupted 3 month march over 3,000 km.

Scott left his base camp on the 1st November 1911, a short time after Amundsen, with 16 men, 10 Siberian ponies, 233 dogs, 13 sledges and trucks, and a set of heavy equipment for scientific observation. At certain intervals small groups left the main column and returned to the base camp, dropping food supplies on their way back in order to secure Scott's return. Very soon the trucks broke down, the ponies had to be slaughtered and the dogs could barely manage to haul the heavy sledges.

On 4th January of 1912, while Amundsen was already on his way back from the Pole, the last auxiliary group left Scott. He continued with a team of four (Bowers, Evans, Oates and Wilson), who hauled the last sledge. With enormous difficulties they finally reached the South Pole on January 17th and discovered they had been preceded by Amundsen. The exhausted and disillusioned Englishmen then started their return journey, but unfavorable weather conditions and food shortage problems prevented their successful return to base camp.

The first to perish was Evans. A few days later Oates left the party's tent and never returned. Violent blizzards forced the remaining three men to stay in their tent for shelter, just 18 km from the nearest food deposit. Scott continued writing his diary, aware that "the end is close... For God's sake, take care of our families." The frozen bodies of Scott, Wilson and Bowers together with their personal effects were found eight months later.

In this way the Antarctic heroic era came to an end and in spite of the shock caused by these dramatic events, the international community celebrated Amundsen's success, made possible by good organization and the choice of adequate equipment.

Shackleton, 1914-15

Shortly after the conquest of the South Pole, the First World War shook the international community and all Antarctic activities were suspended except for a new expedition organized by Shackleton.

The plan of the indomitable Englishman was to cross the continent from the Weddell to the Ross Sea, passing the South Pole. Shackleton left England in 1914 with two ships; he planned to reach the Weddell Sea with the *Endurance* and then to march towards the Pole, while the crew of the *Aurora* was supposed to sail up to the Ross Sea and to proceed towards the Pole organizing food deposits on the way. Unfortunately the *Endurance* was trapped by ice in the Weddell Sea and shipwrecked, with Shackleton and his team just able to disembark onto an iceberg. They spent several months on the drifting block of ice and finally touched land on a deserted island in the South Shetlands. Shackleton eventually succeeded in sailing to the South Georgia Islands in a small boat and in getting help to rescue his companions the following year.

After the end the war, Shackleton organized a new expedition to Antarctica, but he perished after reaching the South Georgias. Since then Shackleton has been remembered as one of the most courageous and tenacious Antarctic explorers, who dedicated his whole life and efforts to the longed-for conquest of Antarctica.

Aeroplane era

Towards the end of the '20s the aeroplane emerged as an important technological innovation which allowed a revolutionary perspective of the continent and opened a new phase in Antarctic exploration. After the initial pioneering stage this new form of transport had a decisive impact on man's expansion into Antarctica, enabling access to the most remote areas and becoming a fundamental logistical support for the settlement of scientific stations on the continent.

The first flight over Antarctica was made in 1928 by the Australian pilot Hubert Wilkins, who flew in a monoplane Lockheed Vega over the Antarctic Peninsula for more than 1,000 km. The following year, after several attempts, Richard Byrd succeeded in flying over the South Pole; in 1935, another American pilot, Lincoln Ellsworth, succeeded in making the first transantarctic crossing by air.

Expansion phase

In 1939 the international scene was completely disrupted by the Second World War and only after 1945 did interest in Antarctica gradually arise again, this time motivated by the possibility of establishing permanent settlements on the continent. Expeditions to Antarctica gradually became more frequent and large-scale; in this context the U.S. Highjump Operation in 1947-48 represented one of the most impressive operations ever undertaken, with the participation of 4,700 men, 13 ships and 24 aircraft.

A growing tendency to assert national presence on the continent was demonstrated by several States which throughout the '50s supported a policy of actual occupation, not always corresponding to scientific objectives. This climate of "Antarctic rush" was also influenced by the international tensions resulting from the cold war between the U.S.A. and the U.S.S.R., which emphasized the strategic importance of Antarctica in controlling southern maritime routes.

International Geophysical Year, 1957-58

These growing concerns alerted the international community which, through the institution of the International Geophysical Year (IGY) in 1957, called for world attention on Antarctica focusing on a scientific and co-operative approach. For 18 months (July 1957-December 1958) scientists of 67 nations co-operated in the largest Antarctic operation ever mounted. In the name of freedom of science, about 50 research stations were built throughout the continent and important scientific results were attained. One of the most successful achievements was the foundation of the Scientific Committee on Antarctic Research (SCAR), an international non-governmental body in charge of co-ordinating scientific activity in Antarctica.

Antarctic Treaty, 1959

The IGY also opened the debate on the political, economic and scientific role of the international community in Antarctic affairs. In 1959 twelve nations which had taken part in the IGY met in Washington to consider the formulation of an international agreement for the management of the continent. The resulting Antarctic Treaty, signed in 1959 by 12 States and later joined by other nations, represented the first co-operative attempt to deal with one of the most sensitive international issues of the modern age.

CHAPTER 7

The legal question
The Antarctic Treaty and other specific conventions

International context

The Antarctic Treaty of 1959 was introduced in a framework of multilateral agreements based on international law drawn up towards the end of the '50s, such as the Conventions on the Law of the Sea (1958), concerning the continental shelf and the high seas besides other issues, and the Outer Space Treaty (1966). These agreements were the result of the appearance on the world map of "new" areas until then out of reach, access to which was made possible by modern technological progress which provided the know-how for their conquest.

Access to areas such as Antarctica, outer space, or the deep oceanic seabed and subsoil raised the question of their administration. The discussion focused on the eventual sovereign rights of individual States and the management of potential exploitation of a scientific, economic or strategic nature. The problem was also to search for an appropriate instrument which could ensure international recognition of any decision made in this context.

On the basis of general principles of law and international custom, and following various recommendations from the U.N. General Assembly, the international community stated its commitment to two fundamental principles. First, it was confirmed that areas of international relevance should not be subject to national appropriation; and second, it was considered that any solution to the problem of international involvement should be examined in conformity with international law in order to obtain its universal recognition.

The result was the drafting of multilateral treaties open to any State willing to accede to them, the main objective of which was to provide the legal framework for a co-operative management of the areas in question and to emphasize their world significance.

Antarctic Treaty

The foundation for an international agreement aimed at regulating the future of Antarctica was laid during the International Geophysical Year (IGY) of 1957-58. In spite of East-West tensions and the open question of territorial sovereignty over Antarctica, the successful results of the IGY led to a worldwide conviction that Antarctica should be accessible to all nations wishing to carry out peaceful activities.

In 1959 an international conference was held in Washington to discuss and define the grounds for an international multilateral agreement. The resulting Antarctic Treaty was approved and signed by 12 States which took part in the IGY: Argentina, Australia, Belgium, Chile, France, Japan, New Zealand, Norway, the Soviet Union, the United Kingdom and the United States of America. The Treaty came into force on June 23rd, 1961 after ratification by all the Signatory States.

Content of the Treaty

The Antarctic Treaty consists of 14 articles, the concise content of which is the following:

ART. I   Antarctica shall be used only for peaceful purposes. Any kind of military activity including manoeuvres and weapon testing are prohibited. Military personnel and equipment may only be employed for scientific or peaceful purposes.

ART. II   Freedom of scientific investigation and co-operationshall continue as during the IGY.

ART. III   Co-operation in scientific investigation shall be promoted through the exchange of information on scientific programs, the exchange of scientific personnel and the exchange of scientific results. Co-operation with international scientific organizations is to be encouraged.

ART. IV   The Treaty shall not be interpreted as a renunciation by any Contracting Party of its rights or claims to territorial sovereignty or as prejudicing its recognition or non-recognition of any other State's rights or claims. While the Treaty is in force, no activity shall constitute a base for asserting or denying a claim to territorial sovereignty nor new claims be asserted.

ART. V   Nuclear explosions and disposal of radioactive waste are prohibited. If international agreements on the use of nuclear energy are concluded and approved by all Contracting Parties, those rules shall then apply.

ART. VI   The Treaty applies to the area south of latitude 60° S including all ice shelves, but it shall not prejudice the rights of any State in conformity with international law in respect to the high seas within that area.

ART. VII   In order to ensure the observance of the Treaty, each Contracting Party has the right to designate national observers with complete freedom of access at any time and to any place to carry out inspections, including aerial observation. Each Contracting Party shall give advance notice of any expedition, station occupation and introduction of military personnel or equipment.

ART. VIII   Observers designated under Article VII and scientific personnel exchanged under Article III are subject to the jurisdiction of the Contracting Party of which they are nationals.

ART. IX   The Contracting Parties shall meet at suitable intervals to exchange information and promote measures aiming at Treaty objectives related to peaceful purposes, scientific research and cooperation, right of inspection, exercise of jurisdiction and preservation of living resources. These meetings are open to any Contracting Party which has become a party to the Treaty and conducts substantial scientific activity, such as the establishment of a scientific station or the dispatch of a scientific expedition.

ART. X   Each Contracting Party shall discourage, compatible with the UN Charter, any activity contrary to the principles of the Treaty.

ART. XI   Disputes between or among Contracting Parties shall be settled by any peaceful means of their own choice (negotiation, mediation, arbitration, etc.). Disputes not so resolved shall be referred with the consent of the Parties to the International Court of Justice for settlement.

ART. XII   The Treaty may be modified or amended at any time by unanimous agreement of the Contracting Parties. After 30 years from the date of entry into force of the Treaty, any Contracting Party may request a conference to review the operation of the Treaty. Any modification or amendment approved by the majority of the Contracting Parties represented at such a conference shall enter into force.

ART. XIII   The present Treaty is subject to the ratification of the Signatory States. It is open for accession to any State which is a member of the UN or is invited to accede to the Treaty with the consent of all Contracting Parties. The Treaty enters into force once all Signatory States have ratified it.

ART. XIV   The United States of America is the depository Government of the present Treaty and shall transmit certified copies to the Governments of the Signatory and acceding States.

Peaceful purposes

As also stated in the preamble to the agreement, the fundamental objective of the Antarctic Treaty is the recognition that the future of Antarctica is an object of concern to all mankind. The statement that Antarctica may be used exclusively for peaceful purposes and must not become the scene of international discord can be interpreted as the fundamental premise for the internationalization of the continent.

In a period in which world equilibrium was strongly affected by international tensions and nuclear development was reaching its maximum expansion, the banning of all military and nuclear activities in Antarctica can be considered an outstanding achievement.

Peaceful purposes

The purpose of peaceful coexistence is reinforced by the principle of freedom of scientific research, promoted through the encouragement of large-scale scientific co-operation. With these provisions the Signatory States have been able to take advantage of objectives pursued in the name of science in order to sidestep major conflicts regarding national jurisdiction over the continent.

Right to inspection

The only restrictions placed on the regime of freedom of science are the obligation to give advance notice of all activities planned by any State and the right to carry out inspections at any time and in any place. These provisions are aimed at guaranteeing the openness of the conduct of individual States and the observance of Treaty principles. The right to inspection in particular is of major significance, as the restriction of the exercise of sovereign rights over national properties such as stations, aircrafts, ships, etc. emphasizes further the principle of internationalization of Antarctica.

Freezing of sovereign rights

It is however universally accepted that the objective of peaceful coexistence is made possible by what is considered a key provision of the Treaty, that is the freezing of all existing claims to territorial sovereignty and of any opposition to them, as well as the non-recognition of new claims while the Treaty is in force. This provision consents the maintenance of a status quo in the dispute over the jurisdictional status of the continent and reflects the desire to postpone the question for an indefinite period, without prejudicing the position of any State.

Claimed sectors

Seven States among the Signatories assert sovereign rights over parts of the Antarctic continent, namely: Argentina, Australia, Chile, France, New Zealand, Norway and the United Kingdom. The United States and the Soviet Union do not recognize the claim of any other State and do not themselves

Claimed Antarctic sectors

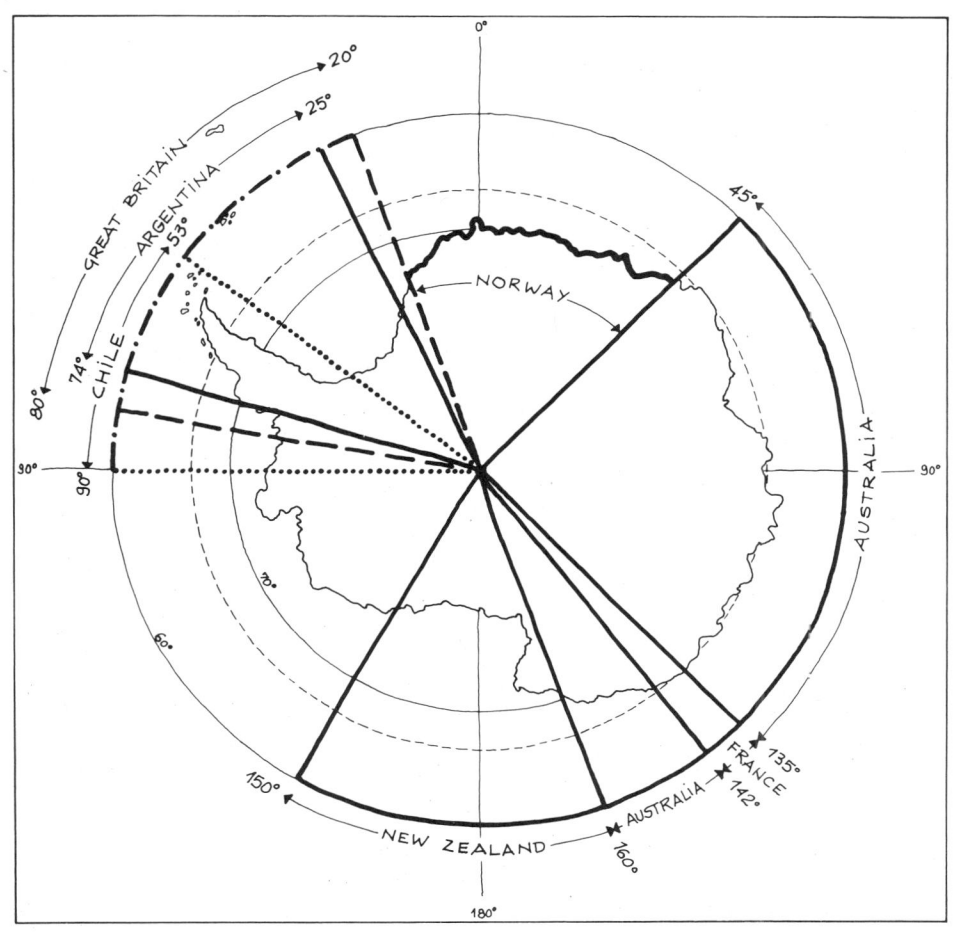

assert any territorial claim, although they have reserved the right to do so at any time. Belgium, Japan and South Africa are the only Signatory States that neither claim sovereign rights nor recognize any claim.

The delimitation criteria of the territories claimed are inspired by the Theory of Sectors, a proposal for territorial division considered at the beginning of this century for the Arctic. According to this theory, the States whose territories extended beyond the Arctic Polar Circle would assert their sovereignty over the area included in a triangle formed by the projection to the North Pole of their western and eastern boundaries.

In the case of Antarctica, the interpretation of the Theory of Sectors was substantially modified. Most States are not geographically adjacent to the continent and the eastern and western limits of the sectors claimed do not always coincide with the projection of the extreme boundaries of each State. The northern limit of all Antarctic sectors coincides with parallel 60° S, except for that of Norway which is not defined. Furthermore Argentina, Chile and the United Kingdom assert sovereign rights over adjacent sectors which partly overlap.

The States asserting territorial sovereignty base their claims on several titles of international law such as priority in discovery, actual occupation, geographical adjacency, and transference of sovereign rights by inheritance, assignment or purchase.

Offshore jurisdiction

The question of sovereignty also opens a sensitive debate on the jurisdiction of individual States over Antarctic offshore zones. In is stated in the Treaty that all provisions apply to the area south of latitude 60° S without prejudicing the rights of individual States over the high seas under international law.

The reference to international law concerns the existing rules established by general principles of law, customary law and international agreements which regulate the conduct of States with respect to the sea. The international law of the sea as now in force allows a coastal State to define a territorial sea area within a limit of 12 nautical miles from its coast, and to exercise sovereign rights over its continental shelf for the exploitation of the natural resources of the seabed and subsoil. States may also declare an Exclusive Economic Zone (E.E.Z.) of 200 nautical miles from their coast, over which they have exclusive rights for the exploitation of marine resources. The zone beyond the E.E.Z. is defined as the high seas and is subject to the legal regime of freedom (freedom of fishing, navigation, prospecting, pipeline laying, etc.).

As far as Antarctica is concerned, the question is whether States claiming sovereign rights could be considered as coastal nations and, consequently, whether their jurisdictional claim could also apply to offshore areas. It is accepted, however, that the principle of freezing all sovereign rights contained in Article IV should be interpreted as applying to the entire area south of latitude 60° S; all Antarctic circumpolar waters up to the continental shoreline and the ice shelves should thus be regarded as high seas and governed by the regime of freedom. This question has an important place in the management of Antarctic affairs since it is commonly supposed that Antarctica's exploitable resources - living and non-living - are mostly concentrated in coastal and marine zones.

Individual claims apart, however, the evolution of present international law is strongly influenced by the growth of an international consciousness about areas such as the high seas, outer space, and Antarctica which progressively tend to be regulated in accordance with the principle of common heritage of mankind. Although the debate is still open, alternative solutions are examined through parallel agreements focusing on specific questions, such as the Convention on the Conservation of Antarctic Marine Living Resources (CCAMLR) and the Convention on the Regulation of Antarctic Mineral Resource Activities (CRAMRA).

Consultative Meetings

The dynamics of the Antarctic Treaty and the realization of its objectives are secured by the principle that Treaty States will meet at suitable intervals to consult together and adopt measures to further the aims of the Treaty. Since 1961 such meetings have been taking place regularly almost every two years and constitute an on-going consultative mechanism which has allowed the Antarctic community to keep up-to-date with impending issues and concerns. In order to update the content of the Treaty, several measures and new agreements on specific matters have also been adopted.

The decision-making mechanism of the Consultative Meetings relies on the advisory function of the Scientific Committee on Antarctic Research (SCAR), an international non-governmental body founded during the IGY in charge of co-ordinating scientific research in Antarctica.

Status of the Parties

Meetings are held by the 12 Signatory States and by those States which have joined the Treaty and have acceded to the status of Consultative Party. The Treaty in fact defines two categories of Contracting Party among the new acceding States: the Antarctic Treaty is open to any State willing to sign (Adherent State), but only those States conducting substantial scientific research, such as the establishment of a scientific station or the dispatch of a scientific expedition, have the right to participate in Consultative Meetings (Consultative States). The main implication of this distinction is that decision-making power is held exclusively by those States recognized as Consultative Parties.

Criticisms of Treaty selectivity

In addition to the 12 original Signatory States, several nations have joined the Treaty since 1959 and some of them have acquired consultative status. In recent years, however, this selective mechanism has become the object of severe criticism from an important sector of the international community.

Member States of the Antarctic Treaty

State	Date of ratification	Status	Change of status	
UNITED KINGDOM	31 May 1960	SS/CP		
SOUTH AFRICA	21 Jun 1960	SS/CP		
BELGIUM	26 Jul 1960	SS/CP		
JAPAN	4 Aug 1960	SS/CP		
USA	18 Aug 1960	SS/CP		
NORWAY	24 Aug 1960	SS/CP		
FRANCE	16 Sep 1960	SS/CP		
NEW ZEALAND	1 Nov 1960	SS/CP		
SOVIET UNION	2 Nov 1960	SS/CP		
POLAND	8 Jun 1961	AS	29 Jul 1977	CP
ARGENTINA	23 Jun 1961	SS/CP		
AUSTRALIA	23 Jun 1961	SS/CP		
CHILE	23 Jun 1961	SS/CP		
CZECHOSLOVAKIA	14 Jun 1962	AS		
DENMARK	20 May 1965	AS		
NETHERLANDS	30 Mar 1967	AS	19 Nov 1990	CP
RUMANIA	15 Sep 1971	AS		
GERMANY (GDR) *	19 Nov 1974	AS	5 Oct 1987	CP
BRAZIL	16 May 1975	AS	12 Sep 1983	CP
BULGARIA	11 Sep 1978	AS		
GERMANY (FRG) *	5 Feb 1979	AS	3 Mar 1981	CP
URUGUAY	11 Jan 1980	AS	7 Oct 1985	CP
PAPUA NEW GUINEA	16 Mar 1981	AS		
ITALY	18 Mar 1981	AS	5 Oct 1987	CP
PERU	10 Apr 1981	AS		
SPAIN	31 Mar 1982	AS	21 Sep 1988	CP
CHINA, PEOPLE'S REP.	8 Jun 1983	AS	7 Oct 1985	CP
INDIA	19 Aug 1983	AS	12 Sep 1983	CP
HUNGARY	27 Jan 1984	AS		
SWEDEN	24 Apr 1984	AS	21 Sep 1988	CP
FINLAND	15 May 1984	AS		
CUBA	16 Aug 1984	AS		
KOREA (SEOUL)	28 Nov 1986	AS		
GREECE	8 Jan 1987	AS		
KOREA (PYONGYANG)	21 Jan 1987	AS		
AUSTRIA	25 Aug 1987	AS		
ECUADOR	15 Sep 1987	AS	19 Nov 1990	CP
CANADA	4 May 1988	AS		
COLOMBIA	31 Jan 1989	AS		

SS: Signatory State
CP: Consultative Party
AS: Adherent State
* 3 Oct 1990: unification of the Federal and Democratic Republics of Germany

Since the conception of the Treaty in the late '50s a decisive role has been played by the developing countries, whose growing political participation has substantially influenced world affairs. Their appearance on the Antarctic scene has emphasized the exclusive character of the Treaty, by which the decision-making mechanism is controlled by a restricted group of States which can afford to sponsor substantial research activities. Their position has grown stronger parallel to the tendency in international law to apply the principle of common heritage of mankind to areas of world relevance.

Their position has also been supported by the growing role played by international institutions such as the UN General Assembly in defining the leading principles for the management of such areas. The first explicit step in this direction was taken in 1983 by the representatives of Malaysia and of Antigua and Barbuda, who proposed that the UN General Assembly include the Antarctic question within the scope of the UN on the grounds that Antarctica should be considered an object of interest for all mankind.

These concerns have also been taken up by several non-governmental organizations specialized in environmental issues. The growing economic interest in Antarctic resources, in particular the possibility of mineral exploitation, has alerted environmentalists concerned about the eventual impact on local ecosystems. They basically criticize the secrecy of Consultative Meetings and demand major openness in all decisions affecting Antarctica.

It has also been emphasized that scientific research carried out in Antarctica involves programs on an increasingly large scale and of an interdisciplinary nature which focus on phenomena of world relevance such as plate tectonics, world climate, ozone, etc.

All these pressures have strengthened the view that Antarctica should become an object of world concern and have determined important changes in the management of the Treaty. The first step in this direction was the decision taken in 1983 by the Consultative States to open Consultative Meetings to Adherent States, and since 1985 representatives of non-governmental organizations substantially engaged in Antarctic scientific activity have also been invited as observers.

Revision mechanism

These changes confirm the view that Antarctica has become a topical subject under constant review, but at the same time underline the great difficulty in attempting to place the Antarctic issue in a legal context which ensures stability and continuity.

The Treaty anticipates this difficulty in its provisions for modification or amendment of its conditions at any time, though only with the unanimous consent of all Consultative States. Further, it states that any Consultative Party may ask for a revision of the Treaty 30 years from the date of its entry into force. This does not imply that after this period the Treaty will expire, but is rather a mechanism aimed at offering to the States the option to reconsider the effectiveness of the agreement and to adopt new measures to improve or update its operation.

The Antarctic Treaty can be considered as the first step taken by the international community towards a delicate balance between internationalization of the continent and the safeguard of national interests. This is reflected in the extreme caution of its provisions, which are nonetheless farsighted enough to secure its future functioning. In this sense a major role is played by the Consultative Meetings at which States can periodically update Treaty objectives and work out new legal agreements.

Recommendations

Since the entry into force of the Treaty more than 150 recommendations have been adopted by the Consultative States. These are common decisions binding for all Treaty States which cover various areas, but are largely related to scientific research and environmental questions.

A major achievement was the adoption in 1964 of the Agreed Measures for the Conservation of Antarctic Flora and Fauna, which represent the first step towards the acceptance of a global environmental policy. They put pressure on the States to restrain from any disruptive activity close to bird or mammal colonies, from the killing, wounding or capture of animals and from the introduction of non-indigenous living species. Accurate lists have been drawn up of Specially Protected Species (SPS) and Specially Protected Areas (SPA) in which scientific activity is also severely restricted. Further recommendations have set aside Sites of Special Scientific Interest (SSSI) as areas to be used exclusively for scientific purposes for a limited period.

Growing concern about man's impact on the Antarctic environment has also led to the adoption of several measures regulating the conduct of expeditions to Antarctica and station activities. Special emphasis has been placed on the question of waste disposal and environmental contamination.

The remarkable increase in commercial tourism and non-governmental expeditions in recent years has led the Treaty States to adopt specific recommendations aimed at regulating such activities and to draw up a Code of conduct for visitors to Antarctica (see Appendix A).

Other recommendations deal with general issues related to transport, communication and logistics, as well as with the functioning of the Treaty and Consultative Meetings.

In several cases recommendations have prepared the ground for the formulation of further international agreements on specific questions and, since 1961, the Treaty States have concluded three more conventions.

Seal Convention (CCAS)

The first international agreement signed under the terms of the Treaty was the Convention for the Conservation of Antarctic Seals (CCAS) of 1971, which came into force six years later. It applies to the area south of latitude 60° S and to all species of seals living within it.

The Convention establishes the complete protection of Fur, Ross and Elephant seals and places severe restrictions on the hunting of other species, such as the setting of annual quotas, catching seasons and areas. It is recommended that seals be killed quickly and humanely, and be taken only on land.

Convention on Marine Living Resources (CCAMLR)

In 1980 the international community adopted the Convention on the Conservation of Antarctic Marine Living Resources (CCAMLR) which came into force in 1982.

The Convention was the result of two basic concerns. First, that fishing carried out in the Antarctic Ocean since the '60s was reaching such uncontrolled levels (especially for finfish and krill) that international attention was drawn to the fact that overexploitation could cause the stocks of determined species to fall below recovery level. Second, with the gradual incorporation of the traditional single-species approach into a much more global perspective based on the concept of the ecosystem, more weight was being given to the belief that the dynamics of individual species could not be fully understood without considering their complex interaction with their habitat and other species sharing the same environment.

This "ecosystem approach" was adopted by the CCALMR, the fundamental objective of which is the conservation and management of the population of finfish, molluscs, crustaceans and all other species of living organisms, including birds, which inhabit the maritime region south of the Antarctic Convergence.

The Convention promotes all efforts to prevent any harvested population from falling below the level which ensures the stability of its population and encourages all efforts directed at avoiding the risk of changes in the marine ecosystem not reversible in the short-term. The principle of rational use of living marine resources is emphasized by the obligation to consider the harvesting of a target species in relation to other dependant populations.

The CCALMR is administered by a Scientific Committee with research and advisory duties, and a Commission in charge of drawing up conservation strategies. Among the conservation measures adopted during the annual meetings of the Commission the most outstanding have been the setting of overall catching quotas, the designation of catching areas and seasons, the complete protection of determined species and zones, and the regulation of harvesting methods.

Mineral Convention (CRAMRA)

The most recent agreement adopted but not yet ratified by all States and therefore not yet in force is the Convention on the Regulation of Antarctic Mineral Resources Activities (CRAMRA) of 1988. It is the result of a six-year round of negotiations conducted by the Antarctic Treaty States with the purpose of finding a joint solution to the mineral question within the legal framework of the Antarctic system.

In the last few decades the intensification of scientific research supported by increasingly sophisticated technologies has suggested the existence of mineral resources in Antarctica. Although the real volume of this potential – both metallic and non-metallic, and in particular hydrocarbons– is still unknown and the adequate technology for its exploitation is not yet available, this issue has turned into one of the most sensitive objects of international debate.

On one side, the "ecosystem approach" has underlined the importance of including also non-living resources in global environmental policies and has emphasized the need to evaluate carefully the future impact of mineral prospection, exploration and exploitation on the Antarctic ecological equilibrium. Non-Treaty States and developing countries have also criticized the CRAMRA on the grounds that mineral exploitation in Antarctica should be discussed in an international forum and should be carried out in the interest of all mankind.

On the other side, the Treaty States have maintained that the issue should be considered within the framework of the Treaty system. This approach, however, has forced them to search for a difficult balance between all the parties involved, namely socialist and non-socialist nations, developed and developing countries, and particularly between States claiming sovereign rights and non-claimant States.

The Convention may be interpreted as a preventive agreement, the main objective of which is to reinforce the peaceful purposes of all Antarctic activities. The scope of its provisions is global and, rather than a detailed mining code, it establishes general requirements for any mineral activity which may take place in the future. Special emphasis is placed on the preservation of the Antarctic environment and it is explicitly stated that no mineral exploitation will be undertaken until appropriate technologies are available and the impact on the local ecosystem is known. The CRAMRA applies to the Antarctic continent and the Antarctic Islands south of latitude 60° S, as well as to the subsoil and deep seabed of their adjacent continental shelf.

The Convention regulates three stages of mineral activities, namely: prospection, exploration and development. No prior authorization is required for the Parties to prospect potential sites. As far as exploration and development are concerned, the CRAMRA Commission will evaluate and eventually authorize an operator's application for a determined area and resource; for each area, a Regulatory Committee will be set up for the purpose of establishing the specific requirements necessary for exploration or exploitation activities. Regulatory Committees consist of several members representing both claimant and non-claimant States and must include the State or States with a territorial claim in the area identified.

CHAPTER 8

Scientific research and human presence in Antarctica

General scientific interest in Antarctica already existed at the time of the very first voyages of discovery to the southern hemisphere, but at that time explorers were concerned primarily with the topographical survey of the region. Towards the end of the last century, the first co-ordinated expeditions of a predominantly scientific nature left for Antarctica, marking the birth of the new discipline of Antarctic science, based on a growing interest in a systematic global approach.

The development of integrated scientific research, however, became possible only in the first decades of the 1900s as a result of the innovations brought about by technological progress. The introduction of modern means of transportation –the aeroplane in particular– and of radiocommunications had a decisive impact on the logistics of Antarctic exploration. They allowed the shift from traditional ship-based to land-based activities, providing the basis for the permanent settlement of man on the continent and the establishment of scientific stations in which systematic research could be carried out.

International Geophysical Year, (1957-58)

After the Second World War the rapid progress made in the field of geophysics and ionosphere studies induced the international scientific community to consider the organization of a new International Polar Year. The forecast that the years 1957-58 would coincide with a period of maximum solar activity, however, offered an opportunity to extend the scope of investigation and to include global geophysical objectives, with particular emphasis on high latitudes. The original idea was thus abandoned in favor of a broader-based International Geophysical Year (IGY).

A Special Committee was set up by the International Council of Scientific Unions (ICSU) to co-ordinate the project. The Committee emphasized the importance of Antarctica within the scope of the IGY and recommended the establishment of stations all over the continent for observation purposes. It was unanimously accepted that any activity carried out in Antarctica had to have an exclusively scientific objective, with no interference from political or economic issues. Scientific co-operation and freedom of exchange of information had to be maintained throughout the IGY.

The IGY began officially on 1st July of 1957 and ended on 31st December of 1958. It saw the participation of 67 nations and several thousand scientists

Member States of the SCAR

State	Date of admission	Status	Change of status	
ARGENTINA	3 Feb 1958	FM		
AUSTRALIA	3 Feb 1958	FM		
BELGIUM	3 Feb 1958	FM		
CHILE	3 Feb 1958	FM		
FRANCE	3 Feb 1958	FM		
JAPAN	3 Feb 1958	FM		
NEW ZEALAND	3 Feb 1958	FM		
NORWAY	3 Feb 1958	FM		
SOUTH AFRICA	3 Feb 1958	FM		
SOVIET UNION	3 Feb 1958	FM		
UNITED KINGDOM	3 Feb 1958	FM		
USA	3 Feb 1958	FM		
GERMANY (FRG) *	22 May 1978	FM		
POLAND	22 May 1978	FM		
GERMANY (GDR) *	9 Sep 1981	FM		
INDIA	1 Oct 1984	FM		
BRAZIL	1 Oct 1984	FM		
CHINA, PEOPLE'S REP.	23 Jun 1986	FM		
SPAIN	15 Jan 1987	AM	16 Jul 1990	FM
SWEDEN	24 Mar 1987	AM	12 Sep 1988	FM
PERU	14 Apr 1987	AM		
ITALY	19 May 1987	AM	12 Sep 1988	FM
NETHERLANDS	20 May 1987	AM	16 Jul 1990	FM
SWITZERLAND	16 Jun 1987	AM		
URUGUAY	29 Jul 1987	AM	12 Sep 1988	FM
KOREA (SEOUL)	18 Dec 1987	AM	16 Jul 1990	FM
FINLAND	1 Jul 1988	AM	16 Jul 1990	FM
ECUADOR	12 Sep 1988	AM		
COLOMBIA	16 Jul 1990	AM		

FM: Full Member
AM: Associate Member
* 3 Oct 1990: unification of the Federal and Democratic Republics of Germany

who worked in more than 2,500 observation stations scattered all over the world. About 50 stations were built in Antarctica by the 12 nations which would shortly after become the signatory States of the Antarctic Treaty. Scientific research focused on geomagnetism, ionosphere physics, auroras, seismology, meteorology, glaciology, oceanography and biology, and furnished a global knowledge of the Antarctic environment, until then fragmented and extremely approximate.

Scientific Committee on Antarctic Research (SCAR)

During the IGY several specialized national and international bodies were created to manage Antarctic scientific programs, but the extreme range of their interests soon demanded the creation of a specific body in charge of co-ordinating scientific research and of furthering international co-operation once the IGY was over.

In 1958, on the basis of a proposal put forward by the IGY Special Committee, the ICSU created the Scientific Committee on Antarctic Research (SCAR). It consisted of the delegates of those States substantially involved in Antarctic research and the representatives of several international scientific institutions. As stated in its Charter, the SCAR is charged with furthering the co-ordination of scientific activity in Antarctica, with a view to framing a scientific program of circumpolar scope and significance south of the Antarctic Convergence.

Any State carrying out substantial research in Antarctica may apply for full membership and may be represented at SCAR meetings by its National Research Committee. States which intend to conduct scientific activities may apply to participate in SCAR meetings as observers, or apply for the status of adherent member. SCAR members meet every two years.

Working groups

For maximum effectiveness the SCAR is subdivided into 10 permanent working groups on general issues: biology, geodesy and cartography, geology, glaciology, logistics, meteorology, oceanography, earth geophysics, high atmosphere physics, and human biology and medicine. At the request of national committees or Antarctic Treaty States, special working groups may also be set up to examine specific questions.

SCAR functions

The co-ordination of scientific research is achieved by the SCAR through its function as a forum in which all members exchange regular information on their activities. Every year, each national committee is supposed to present to the SCAR a detailed report on its past activities and its future programs; in its turn, the SCAR publishes a trimestral bulletin containing general information about meetings, recommendations and resolutions, and members' activities.

The SCAR also plays a fundamental role in the decision-making mechanism set up by the Antarctic Treaty; the Consultative States consider the Committee as their basic advisory source for any scientific issue they have to consider and decide on.

International organizations

Since the late '50s tight co-operative links have been established by the SCAR and the Treaty system with several international bodies. Most of them take part in SCAR meetings and in recent years they have participated as observers in the Treaty Consultative Meetings when specific issues in their field are discussed. Among the most active are:

– WORLD METEOROLOGICAL ORGANIZATION (WMO): one of the first UN agencies involved in Antarctic research, it is in charge of co-ordinating all activities connected with meteorological observation in Antarctica. The WMO established a direct link with the Treaty system through its special working group on Antarctic Meteorology.

– FOOD AND AGRICULTURE ORGANIZATION (FAO): a UN agency which participates in Antarctic research through the program on world fishery, it co-operates with the decision-making and technical bodies set up by the Convention for the Conservation of Antarctic Living Marine Resources (CCALMR).

– SCIENTIFIC COMMITTEE ON OCEANIC RESEARCH (SCOR): a member of the ICSU involved in research programs on marine ecosystems, marine glaciology, and physical and chemical oceanography, it has obtained the status of observer on the CCALMR Scientific Committee.

– INTERGOVERNMENTAL OCEANOGRAPHIC COMMISSION (IOC): part of the UNESCO, it participates in most international programs concerning Southern Oceans and works in conjunction with the Scientific Committee on Oceanic Research (SCOR) and the International Whaling Commission (IWC).

– INTERNATIONAL WHALING COMMISSION (IWC): created in 1946 to regulate indiscriminate whaling, it co-ordinates research on whale populations and is actively engaged in Antarctic activities as an advisory body to the CCALMR Scientific Committee.

Conservation organizations

As a result of growing concern about global environmental issues, several non-governmental conservation organizations have also appeared on the Antarctic scene in the last few decades.

Early environmental movements first appeared at the beginning of this century alerted by the spreading urbanization of the planet and contributed to the development of a new ecological consciousness, founded on the belief that man had both the right to enjoy and make use of nature, and the duty to preserve it for future generations. On this basis the world's first protected areas, National Parks and Reserves were established. Since that time, the conservation lobby has grown increasingly stronger and has gradually acquired decisive political and cultural weight on an international scale, especially since the '60s when it appeared that the development pattern pursued by the industrialized world had to be included in a global environmental policy in order to avoid a major threat to world ecological balance.

In this context, the conservation movement played a major role in highlighting the importance of Antarctica as the last untouched land on earth, and in calling for world attention to the need to preserve its environment and to evaluate carefully the eventual impact of human activities on its ecology. Organizations such as the Antarctic and Southern Ocean Coalition (ASOC), Greenpeace, the World Wildlife Fund (WWF) and many others carry out private research and aim at being internationally recognized as members of the Antarctic scientific community; they also address public opinion through meetings, conferences, and publications. They basically demand greater openness in the management of Antarctica and among their proposals, the most significant are the constitution of a special agency within the UN in charge of the preservation of the Antarctic environment, and the declaration of Antarctica as a world park.

Some conservation organizations are also pressing to be admitted as observers to the committees and meetings set up by the Treaty system; furthermore, Greenpeace demands to be recognized as a Consultative Party to the Antarctic Treaty on the grounds that it runs a permanent station in Antarctica, in which it conducts substantial research activities.

Antarctic stations

Scientific research is carried out in the Antarctic stations scattered all over the continent, which belong to the member States of the Antarctic Treaty.

The first permanent human settlement in the Antarctic region was the observatory built on Laurie Island (South Georgias) by the Scottish expedition of 1902-04 and given to the Argentine government in 1903. In following years several expeditions spent winter months in Antarctica and built huts or camps where they could shelter from extreme weather conditions and   carry out scientific observation, but these were temporary establishments used for specific purposes rather than real settlements. Only after the Second World War did some States consider the possibility of developing a systematic settlement program on the continent, which would allow them both to pursue scientific objectives and to assert actual occupation over determined areas.

Early permanent stations

The first permanent stations were built in the late '40s by Great Britain, Argentina and Chile in the Antarctic Peninsula area and, in the following decade, preparations for the IGY were an incentive for most States to begin building permanent establishments. The majority of the stations were settled along the Antarctic coast, except the American Amundsen-Scott station located at the South Pole and the Russian Vostok station situated in the center of the polar plateau. In the years 1957-58 about 50 stations were operating in Antarctica to pursue IGY objectives.

Once the IGY was over, most nations involved in Antarctica proceeded to reorganize their settlement policies in accordance with their own objectives; some of the IGY stations were dismantled, as in the case of Belgium and Norway, while other States transformed their temporary settlements into permanent stations and built new ones.

Station distribution

The distribution of stations over the continent has corresponded to the occupation policy of each State. States asserting sovereign rights have tended to build their establishments within the sector claimed; the only exception is Norway, which at present has no station of its own. This tendency explains the high concentration of settlements in the Antarctic Peninsula area, where the territorial claims of Argentina, Chile and the United Kingdom overlap.

Conversely, non-claimant States have adopted a widespread distribution policy, according to a general pattern aimed at counterbalancing the exclusive occupation of other States. The U.S.A. and the U.S.S.R. in particular have scattered their stations all over the continent and are the only States to have penetrated the inland polar plateau. Nations such as Australia, France, New Zealand, the United Kingdom and South Africa have also settled in several subantarctic islands.

Station distribution has also corresponded to logistical requirements, and this explains why the great majority of stations are situated along the coast and very few are located inland. The highest station concentration is in the South Shetland Islands and the Antarctic Peninsula region because of its proximity to South America and its relatively light environmental conditions.

Station category

Not all the establishments in Antarctica are inhabited throughout the year, but according to their occupation they may be defined as permanent, summer, temporary or inactive settlements. Those establishments which operate all year round are considered permanent stations, while those operating only during summer months or at intervals are defined as summer or temporary stations.

The category of stations may vary continually according to the occupation needs and research objectives of each State; for example, an inactive settlement may be reactivated in order to carry out a specific task and then closed down again. Also, it is often necessary to carry out work away from the station and thus to settle temporary camps or huts only for the period required. In most cases temporary or no longer usable establishments are abandoned

Main scientific stations in Antarctica

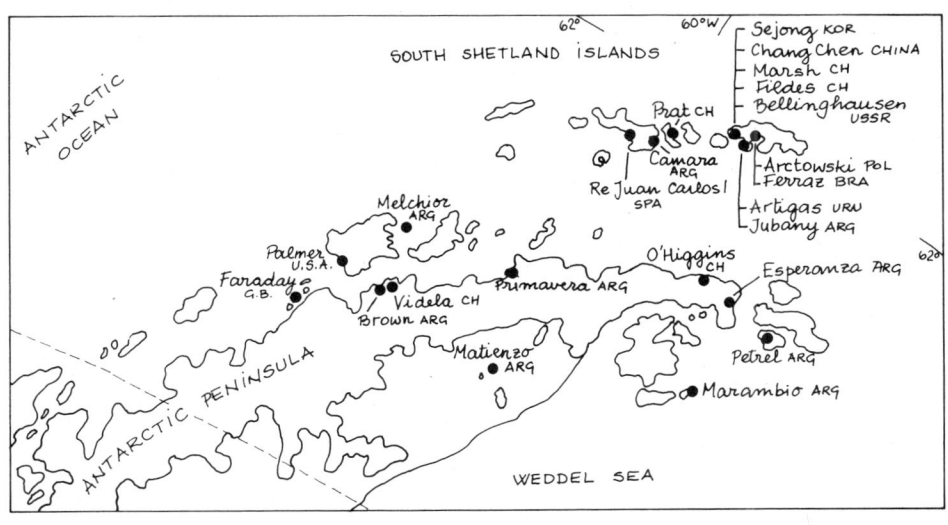

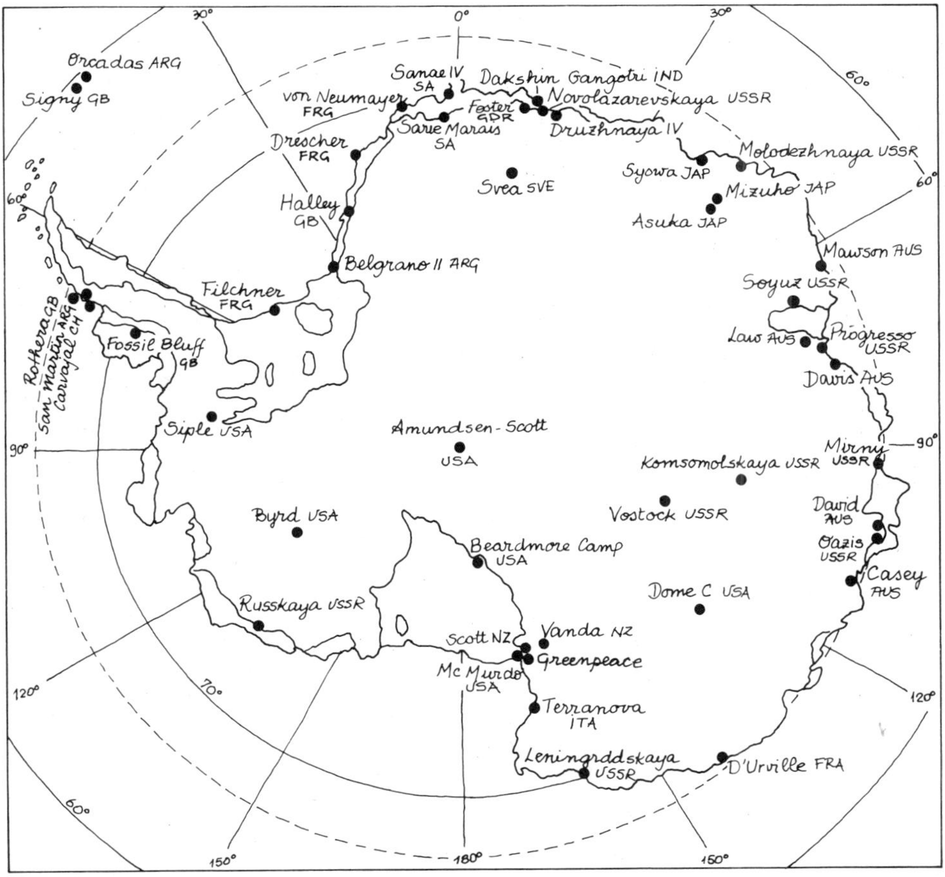

Location of national scientific stations in Antarctica

Station	Latitude	Longitude	Station	Latitude	Longitude
ARGENTINA			**ITALY**		
Belgrano II	77°52' S	34°37' O	Terra Nova	74°42' S	164°06' E
Esperanza	63°24' S	56°59' O	**JAPAN**		
Jubany	62°14' S	58°38' O	Syowa	69°00' S	39°35' E
Marambio	64°14' S	56°43' O	Mizuho	70°42' S	44°20' E
Orcadas	60°45' S	44°43' O	Asuka	71°32' S	44°20' E
San Martin	68°07' S	67°08' O			
Matienzo	64°58' S	60°04' O	**NEW ZEALAND**		
Brown	64°53' S	62°53' O	Scott	77°51' S	166°45' E
Primavera	64°09' S	60°57' O	Vanda	77°31' S	161°28' E
Deception	62°59' S	60°43' O	**POLAND**		
Melchior	64°20' S	62°59' O	Arctowski	62°09' S	58°28' O
Petrel	63°28' S	56°17' O	**SPAIN**		
Camara	62°36' S	59°54' O	Juan Carlos I	62°40' S	62°20' O
AUSTRALIA			**SOUTH AFRICA**		
Casey	66°17' S	110°32' E	Sanae IV	70°18' S	2°25' O
Davis	68°35' S	77°58' E	Sarie Marais	72°02' S	2°48' O
Mawson	67°36' S	62°52' E			
Law	69°25' S	76°13' E	**SWEDEN**		
David	65°51' S	100°30' E	Svea	74°35' S	11°13' O
Commonwealth	67°00' S	142°43' E	Basen	73°02' S	13°25' O
BRAZIL			**UNITED KINGDOM**		
Ferraz	62°05' S	58°23' O	Rothera	67°34' S	68°08' O
Cruls	62°14' S	59°00' O	Halley	75°35' S	26°46' O
Wiltgen	61°13' S	55°21' O	Faraday	65°15' S	64°16' O
CHILE			Signy	60°43' S	45°36' O
Prat	62°30' S	59°41' O	Fossil Bluff	71°20' S	68°17' O
O'Higgins	63°19' S	57°54' O	Damoy	64°49' S	63°31' O
Marsh	62°12' S	58°55' O	**URUGUAY**		
Fildes	62°11' S	58°55' O	Artigas	62°11' S	58°51' O
Carvajal	67°46' S	69°55' O	**U.S.A.**		
Videla	64°49' S	62°52' O	McMurdo	77°51' S	166°40' E
Yelcho	64°52' S	63°35' O	Amundsen-Scott	90°00' S	
CHINA			Palmer	64°46' S	64°03' O
Chang Chen	62°13' S	58°58' O	Siple	75°55' S	83°55' O
KOREA			Beardmore Camp	84°03' S	164°16' E
Sejong	62°13' S	58°45' O	Dome C	74°30' S	123°10' E
FRANCE			Byrd	80°01' S	119°32' O
D'Urville	66°40' S	140°01' E	**U.S.S.R.**		
GERMANY (GDR)			Molodezhnaya	67°40' S	45°50' E
Foster	70°46' S	11°52' E	Mirny	66°33' S	93°01' E
GERMANY (FRG)			Novolazarevsk	70°46' S	11°50' E
von Neumayer	70°37' S	22°08' O	Vostock	78°27' S	106°51' E
Filchner	77°09' S	50°38' O	Bellinghausen	62°12' S	58°58' O
Drescher	72°53' S	19°10' O	Leningradskaya	69°30' S	159°23' E
L. Marleen	71°12' S	164°31' E	Russkaya	74°46' S	136°51' O
Gondwana	74°38' S	164°10' E	Progresso	69°24' S	76°13' E
Greenpeace	77°38' S	166°24' E	Komsomolskaya	74°06' S	97°28' E
			Druzhnaya IV	71°50' S	13°10' O
INDIA			Soyuz	70°35' S	68°47' E
D. Gangotri	70°05' S	12°00' E	Oazis	66°16' S	100°45' E

without being dismantled as such operations are not economically viable. For all these reasons, there are many more establishments in Antarctica than are actually occupied.

Permanent stations and summer settlements of a more permanent character have been increasing in number in the last few years and, at present, number about 50 in total.

Station structure and logistics

The construction features of Antarctic stations are strictly related to the area in which they are built and are of two basic kinds: land-based and ice-based structures.

Land-based stations are built on ice-free soil and consist of several pre-fabricated buildings, sometimes elevated to avoid snow accumulation, which give the settlement the appearance of a small village. They usually include lodgings, common rooms, laboratories, storehouse, energy plant, water deposits, communication room, waste incinerator and workshop, as well as an emergency refuge situated some distance from the other buildings.

Ice-based stations are built following several different techniques. Owing to snow accumulation and subsidence problems, structures are often built underneath the ice and placed in vast cylinders with communicating tunnels; they may be also covered by a geodetic dome, as in the case of the Amundsen-Scott station. These types of station must be periodically checked and rebuilt due to ice movement, which deforms and displaces them.

Two basic sources of energy are most commonly used in Antarctic stations, electric and thermal, which power both the heating of the buildings and all equipment necessary for everyday life and scientific research. Various types of specially treated fuel to resist low temperatures are used, among them diesel fuel, gas oil, and compressed butane and propane gas. In most cases, stations have independent transport and communication links with the State to which they belong and are not connected with each other.

In spite of the sophisticated technology available, the construction and maintenance of a station in Antarctica still requires enormous effort. Apart from the extremely severe environmental conditions, there is no human life-sustaining resource found on the continent except water, and this highlights the fundamental role played by logistical support to Antarctic activities. Station logistics are often managed by the national body in charge of Antarctic activities in co-ordination with their armed forces, which provide necessary technical assistance.

Antarctic population

Human presence in Antarctica is limited to the technical personnel inhabiting the stations scattered on the continent. In comparison with any other inhabited land, this population forms an absolutely singular unit, the main feature of which is its temporary character, as even in permanent stations there is no resident population as staff are periodically relieved.

The population varies substantially throughout the year, with a significant peak in summer months, when most Antarctic activities are carried out. The intensification of summer activities also corresponds to the presence of support personnel operating on ships and aircraft, in many cases more numerous than station inhabitants.

From the establishment of the first stations, the total population increased year by year and reached a relative peak in 1957 during the IGY; in recent years the Antarctic population has averaged out at around 800-1,000 inhabitants during winter months, with an increase to 3,000-4,000 in summer.

The average number of inhabitants per station is quite variable. A typical medium-size station may house up to 40-80 people during summer months; large stations such as the McMurdo (USA), Mirny and Molodezhnaya (USSR), Marambio (ARG) and Casey (AUS) stations often have over 100 inhabitants. McMurdo is the largest of all Antarctic settlements, with a summer population of over 1,000.

The Antarctic population is made up primarily of single adult males, whose average age ranges between 25 and 40. This pattern, however, has gradually changed since the introduction of female staff and family groups including children; women now represent about 15%-20% of Antarctic inhabitants.

The majority of staff are in charge of logistical, general service and technical duties, and the remaining 20%-40% is mainly composed of scientific and a few administrative personnel.

Research fields

Antarctic stations carry out extensive research activities in all traditional scientific fields. In recent decades, however, the general approach has progressively changed from single-sector specialization to a broader interdisciplinary view. This evolution has to a large extent been determined by the development of new technologies which have made possible the study of phenomena previously out of reach technically, such as high atmosphere physics, plate tectonics, paleoclimatology, etc. which, despite their different origins, are believed to interact with each other and should therefore be considered in a global context. The broadening of scientific objectives has also enabled the study of the relationship between Antarctic and world dynamics, making Antarctica a fundamental key to the understanding of world phenomena.

Atmospheric sciences

Special attention has been dedicated to the field of atmospheric sciences, in particular as a result of explicit interest shown during the IGY. Antarctica's location on the South Magnetic Pole and the low absolute humidity and high thermal stability of its atmosphere provide the most favorable conditions for the study of upper atmosphere phenomena such as sun-earth inter-relation, cosmic rays and solar winds, auroras and ionosphere physics, electromagnetism and wave propagation, as well as their impact on telecommunications.

Research is carried out within the scope of the Global Atmosphere Research Program (GARP) and other specific programs, developed at several Antarctic stations in collaboration with the WMO and the ICSU.

Atmospheric studies also allow a better understanding of the eventual impact of human activities on world dynamics. The ozone question is the present object of an international research project set up by NASA and run by several States. The considerable increase in carbon dioxide levels, connected with the so-called greenhouse effect, is carefully monitored by scientists in order to evaluate its impact on world climatic evolution. .

Meteorological observation is carried out at most Antarctic stations and resulting data are analyzed within the general scope of the Research Program on World Climate and, specifically, within the scope of the Research Program on Antarctic Climate.

Important results have also been obtained in the field of paleoclimatology; the analysis of the content of O_{18} in ice samples obtained through deep drilling has provided important information about world climatic evolution in the past 33,000 years.

Glaciology

Since the IGY, basic knowledge about the Antarctic ice sheet has been substantially improved. More accurate information about its volume, shape and thickness has allowed a better understanding of its dynamics and past evolution. Special emphasis has been placed on ice history; the analysis of snow accumulation over time has allowed the reconstruction of paleoclimatic changes for the study of future climatic trends and ice sheet evolution.

Substantial research has been carried out in the field of ice geochemistry, which has provided new information about the structure and age of ice crystals, past atmospheric features and present contamination records.

A substantial part of the research in this field is carried out within global research programs, such as the International Antarctic Glaciology Project (IAGP) and other specific programs conducted jointly by several States.

The influence of sea ice on global climatic and oceanic circulation has highlighted the importance of the investigation of marine glaciology and of iceberg observation; research is carried out in collaboration with the WMO and the specialized working groups of the SCAR.

Earth sciences

Research in the field of earth sciences has been substantially intensified since the IGY, when geophysical studies were declared one of the main objectives of the Antarctic scientific community. As a result of early research activities, it has been possible to obtain basic information about Antarctica's geological structure and subglacial topography, although the geological survey is still being completed at present.

Great emphasis has been placed on the study of the geological history of the continent in order to increase the knowledge of world geodynamics.

Important geochemical and paleomagnetic records have provided substantial evidence in favor of the theory of plate tectonics and continental drift, according to which Antarctica was once a fundamental unit of a larger land mass called Gonwanaland. It has been possible to reconstruct the history of this supercontinent up to several hundred million years ago, and to incorporate its evolution into plate tectonic models.

In recent years, these studies have also been applied to the determination of Antarctica's mineral potential; special attention has been given to the Antarctic continental shelf, where the existence of oil and natural gas is assumed on the basis of geological analogies with other continents formerly adjacent to Antarctica.

Oceanography

Global studies on plate tectonics also apply to the field of oceanography. Research on marine geophysics has focused on global dynamics of the ocean bed and, in particular, on the complex tectonic phenomena which characterize the Scotia Arch and the Antarctic Peninsula area.

Oceanographic research has also involved global studies on oceanic mass dynamics. Physical and chemical studies of the Antarctic Ocean have highlighted its important role in the exchange of polar-tropical waters and in determining thermal and hydric balance on a world scale. Due to the interaction of oceanic and atmospheric phenomena, special attention has been given to the study of global oceanic circulation and its effects on world climatic evolution.

Oceanographic research is carried out by several States in collaboration with the SCOR and the IOC through a global program on Southern Ocean General Circulation, as well as through other specific programs, among them the Antarctic Sea Ice Zone project.

Biology and environmental studies

In relation to oceanographic studies, marine biology is one of the fields of research which have recently stimulated great scientific interest. The Antarctic Ocean is considered one of the most specialized habitats for the study of adaptation processes, fundamental to the understanding of population dynamics and the interrelation of all living species sharing the same environment. The "ecosystem approach" emphasized the need to intensify research on the Antarctic food chain which, from microscopic organisms to large mammals, follows a short and exclusive path based on the high productivity of Antarctic waters.

In this context, the Biological Investigation On Marine Antarctic Systems and Stocks (BIOMASS) has represented one of the most relevant long-term programs on an international scale, aimed at studying the dynamics of the marine ecosystem with a view to achieving a rational administration of Antarctic marine living resources. The BIOMASS has been the result of growing concern about the increasingly large scale harvesting of living resources, particularly of krill, and its impact on the Antarctic ecosystem. The research program has been carried out in two phases, called the First and Second International BIOMASS Experiments (FIBEX and SIBEX) aimed at determining the size and distribution of krill stocks, as well as their role in the Antarctic food chain; other organisms occupying higher food chain levels such as fish and birds were also included.

Biological research in all traditional disciplines is also carried out, with special attention given to evolutionary biology and adaptation mechanisms.

Results in the field of biochemistry have underlined the need to intensify research on the impact of human pollution on living organisms, as a result of the finding of traces of pollutants such as DDT in the fat tissues of penguins, seabirds and seals, as well as in mosses and lichens.

Biomedical studies have been aimed at improving the knowledge of human physiology and its interrelation with the Antarctic environment, focusing on the epidemiology of viral infection, and the physiological and psychological behavior of Antarctic inhabitants.

CHAPTER 9

Antarctic Resources
Past, present and future

Historical background

As a result of its extreme isolation and its recent discovery, Antarctica is undoubtedly the continent least affected by man. Its environmental features and the relative simplicity of its ecosystem, however, make it one of the most vulnerable and high-risk regions on earth, extremely sensitive to any internal and external impact resulting from a human presence and, in particular, from human activities aimed at exploiting its resources.

Historically, interest in Antarctica's economic potential has grown with the expansion of the general knowledge of the continent, favored by modern progress which provided both advanced logistical means and new exploitation technologies.

Early interest in commercial exploitation grew in the first decades of the 1800s, with the easy access to animal resources which led to the appearance of sealers and some years later, of whalers on the polar scene. For the next hundred years exploitation followed very simple patterns, based on the principle that anyone could take any number of seals or whales, with no restriction of any kind and no concern for resource management. With the coming of this century, characterized by targets and needs on a world scale, this specific resource approach was gradually modified. After the Second World War in particular, international interests extended their objectives towards an evaluation of Antarctic economic potential as a whole. A major role was played by the energy crisis which affected the industrialized world in the '70s, underlining the shortage of the basic resources needed to realize its global development program. Renewed interest was thus addressed to Antarctica, focusing on its exploitable potential, in particular for food, energy and water.

International background

The world significance of this perspective raised at the same time the question of the management of Antarctic resources on two basic levels: the management of the benefits of exploitation and the environmental criteria for exploitation.

The first issue is particularly sensitive. The process of internationalization of Antarctica, which began with the signing of the Antarctic Treaty and has since then been reinforced by the growing trend towards the recognition of Antarctica as the common heritage of mankind, has opened the debate on an eventual regulation of economic activities. The question is whether any State may freely exploit any resource on the basis of the traditional principle of freedom, or whether Antarctic resources should be interpreted in a global context of benefit for the whole international community and managed within a regulatory system. This second view is gaining increasingly widespread support as a result of the continuing trend towards the recognition of Antarctica as an object of world concern.

Although the issue is still at present under discussion, special care has been taken to establish exploitation criteria in view of a rational management of present and future Antarctic resources. The growing weight of global environmental policies has played a major role in emphasizing the importance of the "ecosystem approach", according to which an accurate knowledge of environmental dynamics must precede any kind of economic exploitation. In this way, the traditional distinction between renewable and non-renewable resources has also been substantially revised; renewable resources may become non-renewable not only through direct stock depletion, but also as an indirect result of the exploitation of other interdependent resources or environmental damage.

Sealing

The first commercial activity in Antarctica was sealing, which began around 1820 and involved companies from several nations. After depleting the stocks along the coasts of South America, sealers headed south as far as the northern region of the Antarctic Peninsula in search of new exploitable sites.

They were interested primarily in Fur seals, for the high commercial value of their fur, and Elephant seals, for their substantial yield of fat. Both species were harvested so extensively that within a few years their stocks reached near extinction level. In the year 1821-22 more than 300,000 animals were slaughtered in the South Shetland Islands and by 1830 sealing had decreased sharply due to the depletion of stocks. After two renewed peaks, the first between 1870 and 1880 and the second at the beginning of this century, sealing in the Antarctic region ceased almost completely, allowing the slow recovery of the remaining population.

Sealing is at present regulated by the Convention for the Conservation of Antarctic Seals (CCAS), which establishes the total protection of Fur, Ross and Elephant seals and sets an annual maximum catch of 190,000 Crabeater, Weddell and Leopard seals.

Whaling

Whaling has been the most profitable commercial activity in Antarctica, but also the most relentless, with the most disastrous ecological consequences ever witnessed.

Whales have been hunted by indigenous maritime populations since prehistoric times, but only after the 16th century did they become an object

World whale catches in the 1900s

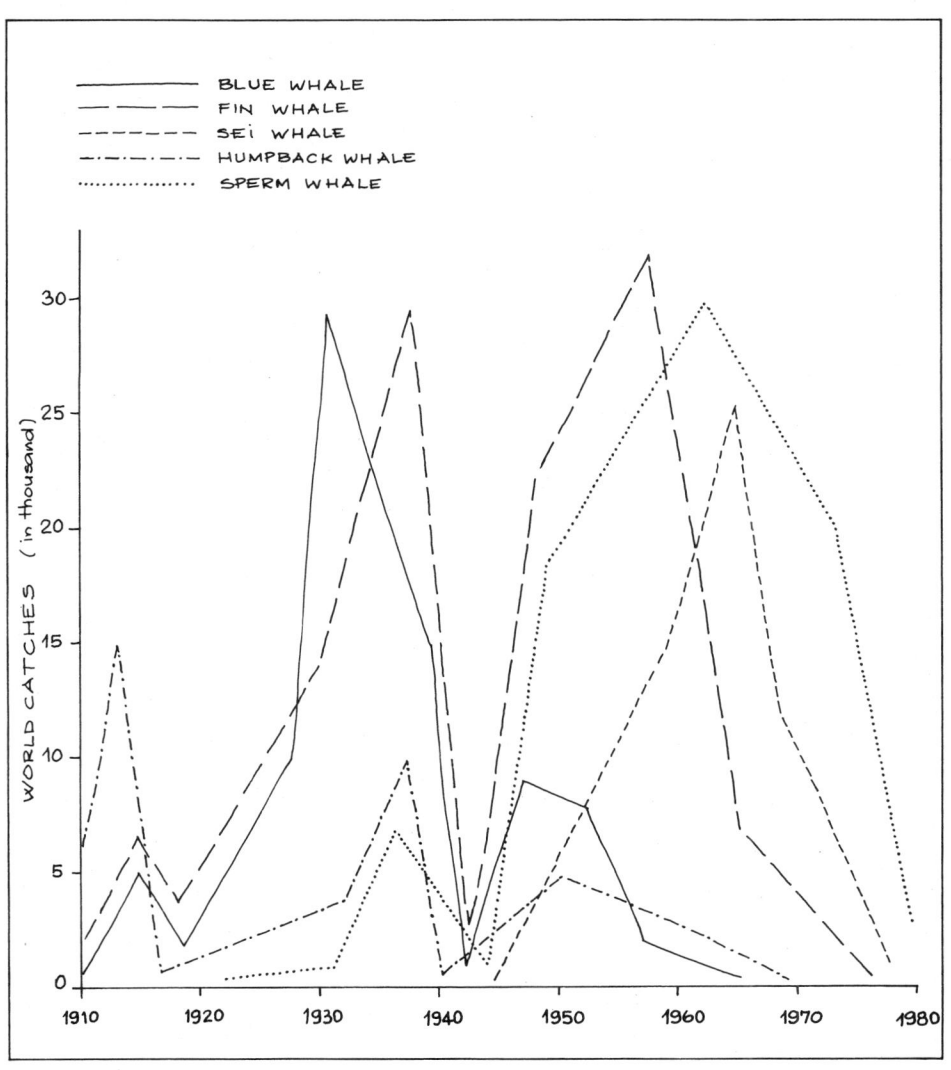

of economic interest for their baleens and their enormous fat content. In the northern hemisphere whaling developed progressively from a pioneer activity into a systematic commercial exploitation which, towards the second half of the 19th century, led to a serious depletion of existing stocks. Whalers then turned their attention to the virtually untouched stocks of the Southern Ocean and shortly after moved into the Antarctic region.

The first land factory was established in the South Georgia Islands in 1904 and, from that time, whaling became increasingly large-scale in operation. It was made more efficient by the adoption of new hunting aids such as the harpoon gun and by factory ships, which allowed extensive hunting saving time and effort.

Hunting pattern

The whalers' hunting pattern was relatively simple. In search of maximum profits, they hunted the largest and most valuable species until its scarcity made the operation unprofitable; they then switched to the next species below it in commercial value, and again hunted it until depletion. Thus, in the early 1900s, the Humpback whale was the hunters' primary target, as world stocks of Right whales had already been decimated before the beginning of Antarctic whaling. In the '20s the Blue whale took its place and, until the '50s, became the object of a relentless and extensive persecution which brought its population to the edge of extinction. Next, it was the turn of the Fin whale, which from the '30s constituted more than 50% of the total annual catch, then gradually substituted by Sei, Minke and Sperm whales in the '60s.

Annual catch

Since the introduction of Antarctic whaling the total annual catch has steadily increased from less than 10,000 whales at the beginning of the century to 20,000 in the '20s and over 40,000 in the '30s. Whaling was practically abandoned world-wide during the Second World War, but increased again immediately after and reached a peak of over 60,000 whales per year in the '60s. As a result of both global stock reduction and growing conservation pressures, whaling began to decrease in the years following and has dropped to a current annual average catch of less than 10,000.

Whaling consequences

Whaling in the Antarctic Ocean has had a disastrous impact on total whale stocks which, in some cases, have been reduced to just 3%-5% of their original number. Special attention has been given in recent years to the study of the present southern population in order to determine its size and, in particular, to establish whether it has dropped below recovery level. It is an extremely difficult task made more so by the fact that whales are confined to the most remote oceanic areas and spend most of their time submerged in deep waters. Much information is still needed, in particular on pre-exploitation stocks, to carry out comparative studies and increase the understanding of the response of whale populations to exploitation. In any case, many more years will be necessary to determine on an evolutionary time scale what mechanism whales have adopted to counter population reduction, if any.

Another important question in the consideration of any possible recovery of whale stocks is their place in the Antarctic ecosystem, and the interaction with food availability and other species feeding on the same resources. For example, since the depletion of whales there has been clear evidence of an increase in other krill eating species, especially Crabeater seals and penguins. The impact of such changes on whale population dynamics, however, is still an open question.

International Whaling Commission

All these issues have become the concern of the International Whaling Commission (IWC), the international body in charge of regulating whale exploitation. In 1946, whaling and non-whaling States met in Washington at an international conference to evaluate the impact of growing exploitation; the result was the adoption of the International Convention for the Regulation of Whaling, which created the Commission.

Among the most significant results achieved since then by the IWC are the total protection of species threatened by extinction and the establishment of exploitation criteria for other species, such as the setting of catch quotas, areas and seasons. The Right, Blue, Humpback, Fin and Sei whales are now protected species, with Minke whales subject to restricted exploitation for scientific purposes only.

In spite of these conservation measures, the effectiveness of the IWC has been severely obstructed by the strong pressure exerted by whaling member States, among them Japan, the Soviet Union and Korea. However, the growing weight of the conservation lobby and the accession to the IWC of an increasing number of non-whaling States have influenced international opinion. An important achievement was the recommendation adopted in 1972 by the UN Conference on Human Environment which pressed for a 10 year moratorium on commercial whaling; the moratorium was eventually passed in 1982 by the IWC, which called for a whaling suspension in order to study its effect on the whale population.

Marine living resources

In spite of the almost complete cessation of sealing and the gradual decrease in whaling, man has continued to focus his attention on the high productivity of the Southern Ocean. The overexploitation of world fish stocks and the increasing demand for proteins led several nations to look at the Antarctic Ocean as a major source of food. Early interest in marine resources arose in the '60s and, since then, finfish and krill have become the object of large-scale fishing by several countries.

Areas of highest krill concentration in the Antarctic Ocean

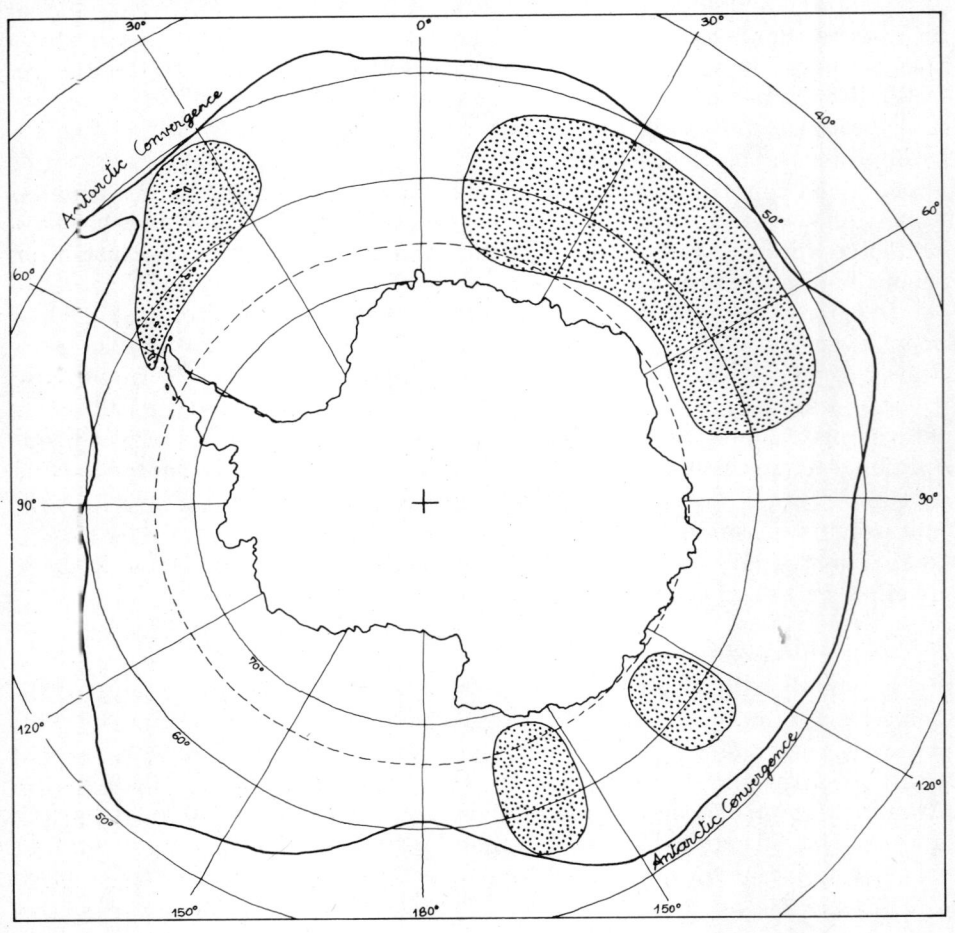

Finfish exploitation

During the early stages of Antarctic fishing, targets included cod-like species of the family *Notot99henia*, in particular the Antarctic cod (*N. rossii*); towards the end of the '70s, the icefish (*Champsocephalus gunnari*) also became the object of intensive exploitation. Fishing was carried out mainly in the waters close to the Kerguelen, South Georgia and South Orkney Islands. The annual fishing catch stood at around 4,000 tons in the early '70s and increased steadily up to a peak of 500,000 tons in the 1979-80 season.

Impact of fishery

Concern about such uncontrolled exploitation together with the pressing need for a global management of southern living resources led to the adoption in 1980 of the Convention for the Conservation of Antarctic Marine Living Resources (CCALMR). Reports to the CCALMR Commission warned in the early '80s that the fish stocks in the South Georgia area were severely depleted, with a 40% total decrease in respect to original size and close to 95% for certain species; other surveys also confirmed the depletion of the two main target species. This situation led the Commission to adopt more severe provisions aimed at prohibiting the fishing of Antarctic cod in the most depleted areas, establishing global catch limits and regulating fishing methods.

Finfish exploitation in Southern waters is too recent to permit an evaluation of its impact on the Antarctic ecosystem. The outlook for a reasonable management of fish resources appears optimistic, however, as major fishing nations such as the U.S.S.R., Japan, China, the U.S.A and Chile have all acceded to the CCALMR.

Krill exploitation

Krill is the other marine living resource which has recently attracted world attention for its high protein content and its abundance. Krill harvesting began in the early '70s with the first experimental fishing carried out by the Soviet Union and Japan, later followed by several other nations. Fishing countries are still at present developing appropriate technologies for its profitable exploitation, as krill presents several problems connected with its rapid deterioration and its high fluor content.

Harvesting volumes

Krill exploitation increased from an annual catch of 20,000 tons in the early '70s to an average of 400,000-600,000 tons in the '80s. The U.S.S.R. is the major krill fishing nation, with a catch of over 350,000 tons in the 1985-86 season; next is Japan, which harvests about 50,000 tons per year, followed by Chile, East Germany, Poland and Korea with much lower average catches of 5,000 tons.

Growing commercial interest in krill has alarmed the scientific community, which through the CCAMLR and other research programs such as the

BIOMASS has emphasized the need to build a solid scientific foundation on which to base any management decision on Antarctic living resources. Special attention has been given to the study of the position of krill in the Antarctic food chain, in order to determine the impact of its exploitation on the local ecosystem.

Present stocks

One of the major concerns of the investigation has been the evaluation of Antarctic krill stocks, a task made quite difficult by their uneven distribution and swarming behavior. As a result of hydroacoustic surveys carried out within the scope of the BIOMASS program, krill stocks have been estimated to vary at between 250 and 700 million tons (annually renewable), but the figure is still quite approximate. Other aspects of the study have related to krill distribution in the Antarctic Ocean, and whether higher areas of concentration correspond to a single breeding population with a high distribution range, or to separate stocks.

Krill surplus

In order to determine whether the productive process of the Antarctic Ocean generates a krill surplus, research has also been aimed at evaluating annual krill consumption by dependent species. Estimates are still at present extremely vague and cautious: seals (with a high preponderance of Crabeater seals) 60-130 million tons; birds 10-130 million tons; whales 40-60 million tons; fish and squid 100 million tons.

The analysis of these results has opened the debate on whether, to what extent, and where an eventual krill surplus could be exploited by man without disastrous ecological consequences. Proposals have varied from cautious figures averaging around a few million tons up to about a 70 million ton annual catch, almost equivalent to the volume of world annual fishery. The hypothesis according to which man could exploit the krill surplus left by the decline of the whale population has been reconsidered; further research will be necessary to increase the understanding of population dynamics of krill dependent species in order to determine to what extent this surplus has already been absorbed by other krill predators.

Mineral exploitation

One of the most topical Antarctic issues is the economic future of the continent as far as non-living resources are concerned. The pressing search for new sources of energy, in particular after the international oil crisis of the '70s, led to special interest in Antarctica's mineral potential.

Hypothetical resource

Geological prospection programs carried out since the '60s have detected the presence of most metallic and non-metallic minerals, but there is as yet no evidence of sufficiently large deposits to make exploitation commercially

Areas of highest mineral concentration in Antarctica

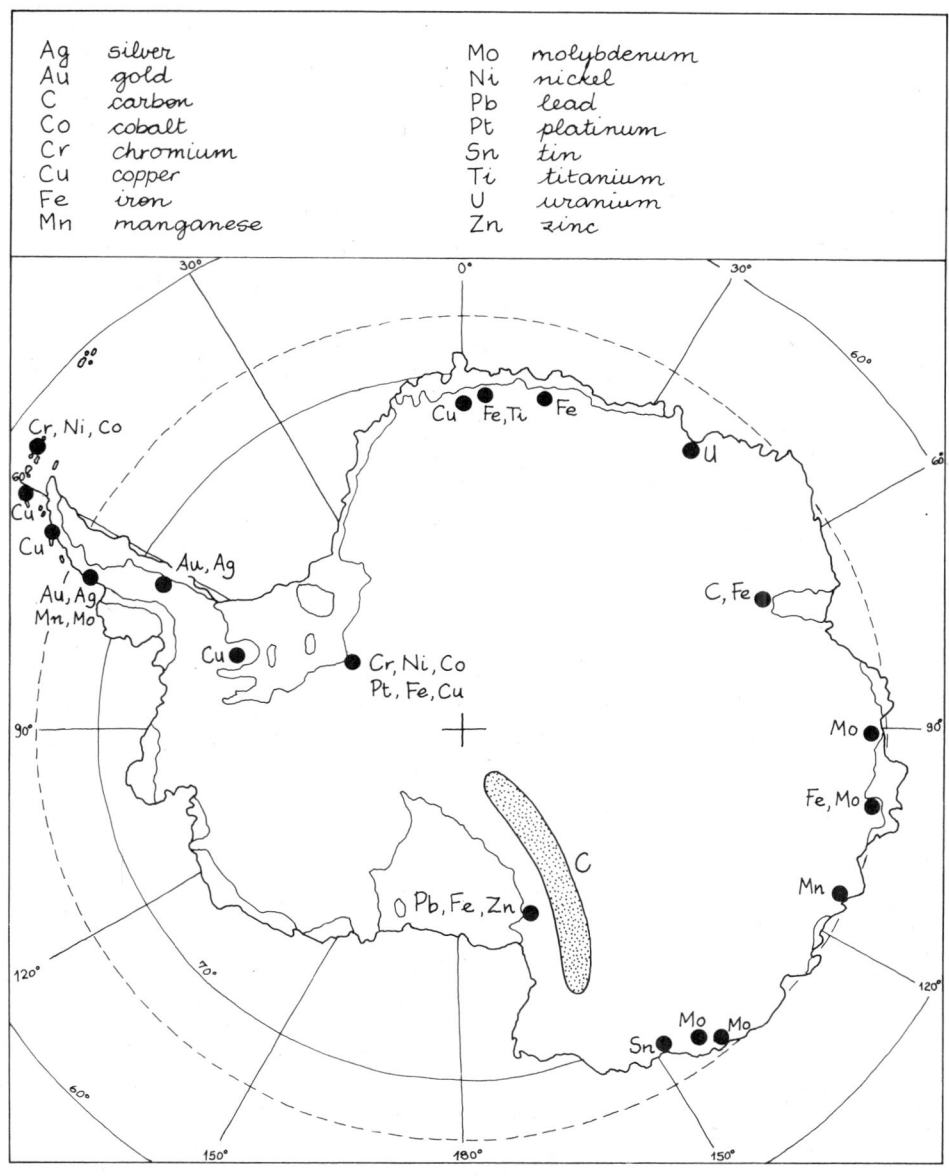

Ag silver   Mo molybdenum
Au gold   Ni nickel
C   carbon   Pb lead
Co cobalt   Pt platinum
Cr chromium   Sn tin
Cu copper   Ti titanium
Fe iron   U   uranium
Mn manganese   Zn zinc

attractive. The need to develop an appropriate mining technology implies such high costs that they could be justified only by huge mineral concentrations, ensuring profitable extraction. For this reason Antarctic mineral potential is generally regarded as a "hypothetical resource", of which hydrocarbons (oil and gas) appear to offer the greatest prospect for future exploitation.

Prospecting methods

The hypothesis of the existence of mineral deposits relies to a great extent on the study of geological analogies between Antarctica and other continents, the margins of which were adjacent to Antarctica at the time of the supercontinent Gondwanaland. On the basis of comparative research important parallels have been drawn between several mineral areas; one example is the geological similarity between the Dufek Massif in the Pensacola Mountains and the Bushveld mineral complex in South Africa, which could suggest that the Dufek region is a potential mineral deposit. Analogies have also been drawn to locate potential hydrocarbon fields by comparing the sedimentary basins of formerly adjacent continental margins and actual producing fields in Australia, South Africa and South America. Although this method may be considered an important guide-line for prospection, it does not guarantee the location of Antarctic mineral sites, as since the early fragmentation of Gondwanaland over 200 million years ago, the geological evolution of all continents has followed different paths.

Metals

As far as the existence of metals is concerned, it is considered that the crystalline shield of East Antarctica, and particularly the Precambrian rocks are the most favorable areas for the presence of metals, as well as the Mesozoic and Cenozoic rocks in the Antarctic Peninsula.

Prospection has detected the presence of copper, iron, zinc, lead, nickel, silver, gold, molybdenum, manganese, cobalt, uranium, titanium, and other metals. Most mineral deposits, however, appear to be very limited and scattered throughout the continent, thus reducing their potential profitability.

Coal

Extensive seams have been detected in the Transantarctic Range region and in Prince Charles Mountains, though they do not appear to be very deep and the coal is generally of low quality. These factors, together with the severe climatic conditions at present make the prospect of profitable exploitation very slight.

Hydrocarbons

The detection of methane and ethane as a result of prospection by the United States in the Ross bay in 1973 focused world attention on the possible existence of hydrocarbons in Antarctica. Since then, growing interest has shown in research programs in the field of petroleum geology.

Sedimentary basins in Antarctica

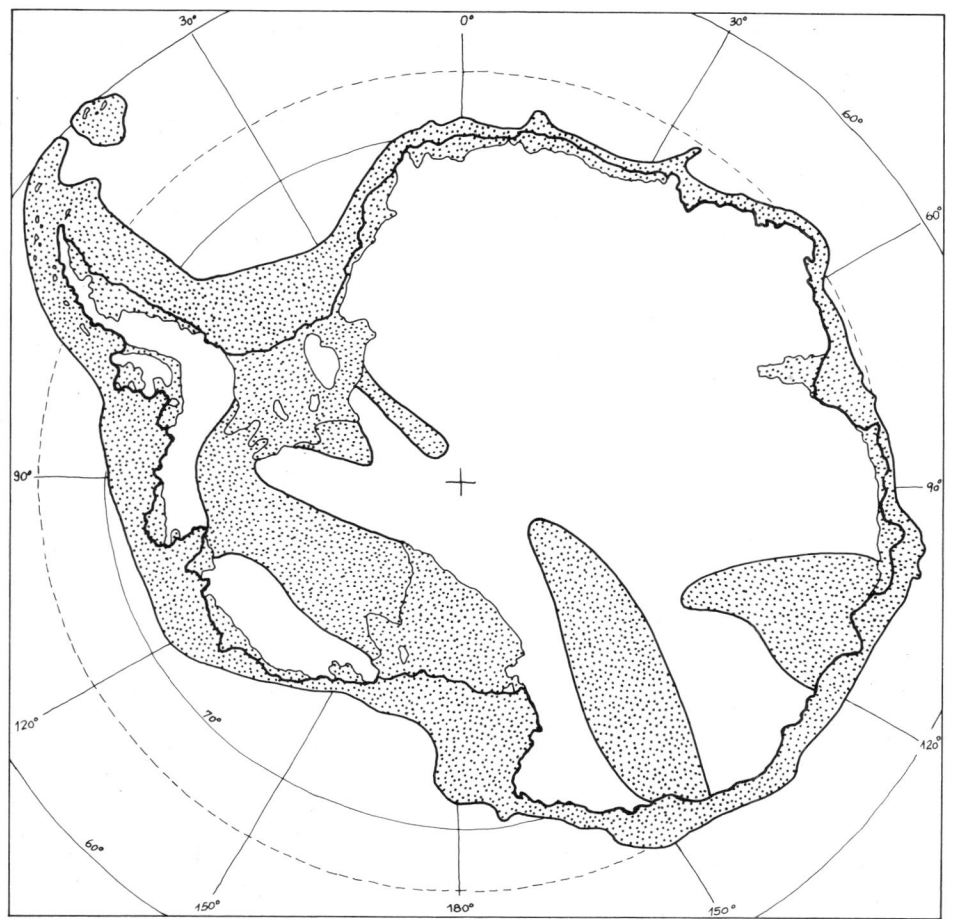

Sedimetary basins

Research has focused on the study of sedimentary basins, considered to be the most suitable geological environment for oil and gas formation. Hydrocarbons are produced through the sedimentation of marine and terrestrial organic debris which, through a combination of time and temperature, undergo transformation processes. Once they have formed, they tend to seep away and to accumulate in close reservoirs sealed by an impermeable cap rock which prevents their leakage. The largest Antarctic sedimentary basins are located along the continental margin, and in particular in the Ross and Weddell bays, though they are also believed to exist in other inland areas.

Exploitation requirements

It is universally accepted, however, that even if the presence of hydrocarbons should be confirmed, exploitation could be envisaged only if fields were large enough to justify the high technological costs implied. Furthermore, an eventual mining development in Antarctica would have to meet several technical requirements, to a large extent still inaccessible. The relative depth of the Antarctic continental shelf (600 m against a mean average of 200 m) would involve deep drilling for which current technologies are still being developed; marine mining platforms would be at continuous risk from drifting pack ice and icebergs, which could cause accidents with disastrous effects on the local environment.

Ice exploitation

Among the Antarctic stocks of non-living resources, ice represents the largest source of freshwater on earth. The exploitation of the huge tabular icebergs which break away from the Antarctic ice shelves has recently been considered as a possible solution to the water problems of arid regions. To give an idea of the amount of freshwater an iceberg could provide, a block of ice measuring, for example, 10 km by 10 km and 100 m thick is equivalent to 10,000 billion liters of fresh water, and the average water consumption of a town-dweller is about 100,000 liters per year.

The proposal for ice exploitation consists of securing large icebergs and towing them with specially equipped ships to a location at which they could be broken into fragments and melted. This operation presents several problems such as the securing of icebergs large enough to justify the high costs involved, their fixing and transport through unfavorable sea currents and winds, their partial melting and their environmental impact during the crossing of temperate regions, as well as their final use. Optimism for the proposal has been generated, however, by the sighting of drifting icebergs a short distance from the Tropic of Capricorn, underlining the important role sea currents could play in facilitating their transport.

Tourism

In recent years tourism has become a new commercial activity in Antarctica. The first pioneer tourist trips were undertaken in the '50s and over time have increased in number and become more structured; it has been estimated that by the '80s more than 20,000 tourists had already visited the continent, and present figures average at around 3,000-4,000 visitors per year. Tourists travel to Antarctica with organized tours either by air or by ship, as well as on private adventure expeditions. Most visits are made to occupied scientific stations and are concentrated in the more easily accessible regions, such as the Antarctic Peninsula, the Ross Island and the Victoria Land area, though exclusive journeys to the South Pole have also been organized.

The recent increase in tourism together with the growing concern about the environmental impact of an uncontrolled development of the "tourist industry" have opened a sensitive debate on its appropriateness and its regulation. Special attention has been given to the issue, especially given the occurrence of several accidents during excursions to Antarctica (in particular the tragic crash on Mount Erebus in 1979 with the loss of 257 lives) and the prejudicial effects on the scientific work of stations which frequent visits of large groups of visitors may cause.

Regulation of tourism

The Antarctic Treaty States, supported by conservation organizations, have issued several recommendations for the management of tourism in Antarctica, concerning the liabilities of both tour operators and visitors. Special emphasis has been placed on the need to give advance notice of any non-governmental expeditions to Antarctica, to exert every effort to ensure that visitors do not engage in any activity contrary to Treaty principles, to ask for previous permission to visit any station and to accept any restriction imposed by the station commander during the visit. Visitors must also be aware of the provisions adopted by Treaty States concerning the protection of flora and fauna, specially protected areas (SPA) and species (SPS), the protection of historic monuments and the procedures for waste disposal. Recommended rules for visitors are contained in a specific code of conduct entitled "Guidance for visitors to the Antarctic" (see Appendix A).

CHAPTER **10**

The environmental question
A challenge to mankind

Ecosystem fragility

From an ecological point of view the Antarctic ecosystem is often referred to as one of the most fragile on earth, but to better understand this view a basic point should be clarified.

Antarctica's fragility is not intrinsic, but is related rather to its interaction with external phenomena. In fact, *within the parameters of its own evolution*, the Antarctic ecosystem is very strong, capable of surviving in the most extreme and isolated habitat. Its equilibrium has been reached through thousands of years of adaptation and specialization processes which have led to the development of local endemisms, or forms of life specially suited to a determined environment. This evolution has produced an ecosystem consisting of a limited number of highly specialized species, the organization of which relies on a high degree of direct dependence on each other and on basic environmental agents. Such an ecological pattern is not *per se* synonymous with fragility, but it does make the whole system particularly sensitive to any external influence which might interfere with its own parameters. In this sense, the Antarctic Convergence marks the natural limit of a well-separated habitat, the ecological isolation of which acts as a kind of self-protection.

Ecosystem organization

The structure of the Antarctic ecosystem is reflected in the organization of its food chain. The trophic system is characterized by a linear and direct relationship between the three levels which include the whole evolutive range: micro-organisms, krill and upper fauna. Any alteration, particularly at the lowest levels, could imply a threat not only to those organisms directly involved, but also to all other dependent species, often specialized on a single prey.

Krill is believed to have a fundamental function in the whole economy of Antarctic marine life; it is the bottle-neck in this organization and consequently influences the development pattern of dependent species.

The upper fauna also represents a community of living organisms the ecology of which is particularly sensitive to any alteration. Any direct threat to their stocks implies far-reaching consequences on their population dynamics, governed by long-term breeding patterns. Penguins, seals and particularly whales have a minimum 12 month reproduction cycle, and with the exception of some species of penguin, they only breed one pup or calf per year.

Their demographical pattern is appropriate for the ecosystem to which they belong, but could become a conditioning factor if any external interference should occur.

There is, furthermore, a tight interrelation between the living community and the Antarctic habitat, which underlines the absolute need to preserve the environmental equilibrium in order to allow the survival of all Antarctic forms of life.

World relevance

The great importance of the ecological dynamics governing the Antarctic environment demands their interpretation in a global context. In fact, Antarctica performs a function that goes beyond its local limits and has a significant influence on parameters related to world ecological equilibrium, such as oceanic and atmospheric circulation, world thermodynamics, etc. The fundamental interaction between Antarctic and world ecosystems, and any impacts on them, can clearly be seen. In this sense Antarctica represents an important touchstone for both local and external alterations, and its virtually untouched environment is ideal for the monitoring of the evolutionary trends of world variables.

Local impacts

The major risks of local interference with the Antarctic ecosystem are undoubtedly related to human presence on the continent, and past experience has demonstrated that uncontrolled exploitation can have far-reaching and disastrous consequences. At present, great emphasis is placed on the need for an extensive knowledge of environmental dynamics before undertaking any commercial activity. This view has been reinforced by the prospect of eventual mineral exploitation, the highest-risk enterprise ever envisaged in Antarctica.

Station impact

Great attention has also been given to the growing urbanization of the continent and its environmental impact. The need to adopt general regulations about the establishment and functioning of stations has been emphasized, in order to avoid research activities becoming a potential threat. Aspects related to station maintenance, such as energy production, waste disposal and logistical support, have been a source of particular concern.

Adopted measures

In the last few years, the SCAR has carried out specific surveys, the results of which have been published in several reports on "Man's impact on the Antarctic environment". These documents provide a global analysis of present human activities affecting the Antarctic ecosystem and recommend several precautionary measures with special attention to the question of waste disposal. The SCAR's concerns have also been adopted by the Consultative States of the Antarctic Treaty, and have led to the publication of a code of conduct for Antarctic expeditions and station activities.

Waste disposal

The question of waste disposal is perhaps the most pressing daily problem faced by all stations. Practices such as open burning of combustible waste, discharge of any liquid waste into the sea, dumping of waste along the shoreline, and the non-removal of plastics, batteries and rubber products from Antarctica are still common in spite of specific recommendations issued by Treaty States.

Logistical risks

Logistical support to research activities and station maintenance also represents a source of environmental risk, in particular owing to the severe conditions with which transport operations have to contend. Although logistical engineering has greatly improved, accidents such as plane crashes or shipwrecks are not uncommon and show that major caution and insurance measures must be taken when operating in the region.

Energy production

There are also environmental risks associated with the production of energy in scientific stations, as the transport and use of fuels represents a potential danger if a spill were to occur. Experience in the use of nuclear energy has demonstrated the high risks involved in such installations; a small nuclear reactor installed in the McMurdo station had to be dismantled after operating problems and more than 10,000 cubic meters of radioactive material had to be shipped back to the United States.

External impacts

In recent years the most serious threats to the environmental stability of Antarctica appear to have come not only from local interference, but also from external variables of world significance, such as contamination and global climatic and atmospheric changes. Most of these phenomena are the result of man's activity and affect the evolution of the whole planet, but their impact on Antarctica can be particularly dangerous, as major alterations to the Antarctic environment could in their turn have far-reaching implications on a world scale. This emphasizes the importance of including Antarctica in world environmental programs, making it clear that no local conservation policy will be effective if it is not included in the global context of preservation of world ecological equilibrium.

Contamination

The detection in the '60s of traces of DDT in the fat tissue of penguins opened a new field of research concerned with the study of environmental contamination. Antarctic ecotoxicology aims at investigating local pollution levels and at deducing from them general information about contamination on a world scale. Though in small amounts, traces of pollutants such as hydrocarbons and its derivatives, products of chemical synthesis, pesticides and DDT have been detected in living organisms and ice samples, confirming the transfer of pollutants produced in industrialized countries through atmospheric circulation. DDT is undoubtedly the pesticide used most extensively in the past few decades and, through the study of its concentration in ice samples, it has been estimated that over one thousand tons has been deposited over Antarctica.

Greenhouse effect

Among the world phenomena considered to be particularly dangerous for the Antarctic environment is the so-called greenhouse effect. This phenomenon is related to the production of carbon dioxide (CO_2), which in the last few decades has risen substantially as a result of increasing combustion processes to produce energy.

Under normal circumstances, the CO_2 contained in the atmosphere is absorbed by plants through photosynthesis, while phytoplankton and other marine organisms absorb the carbon dioxide dissolved in sea water. However, the present overproduction of CO_2, together with the drastic reduction of green areas on earth has generated a surplus which cannot be totally absorbed by natural agents, already at saturation levels. The resulting accumulation of carbon dioxide in the atmosphere has a substantial influence on earth-sun dynamics. Part of the solar radiation which is normally reflected back into space by the earth's surface is now absorbed by the high concentration of CO_2, thus reducing the heat dispersed by the planet.

Consequences

The direct consequence in Antarctica of a progressive increase in the earth's average temperature would be the gradual melting of the ice sheet, which would result in the raising of sea levels and the submersion of coastal areas with obvious disastrous effects. Recent studies have estimated that an increase of 5°C could be sufficient to cause the melting of the West Antarctic ice sheet and the consequent rise of the sea of 5-7 meters above its present level.

Ozone question

The presence of ozone in the highest layers of the atmosphere and its property of absorbing UV solar radiation were already known early this century. About 50 years ago specialists began to carry out ozone measurements and, with improvements in technical instruments, the first variations in ozone concentration were detected. Since the '70s in particular, an important decrease in ozone level has been monitored and the decreasing trend has been confirmed by further observations carried out during the '80s. Land monitoring from Halley Bay in Antarctica and aerial monitoring by the NASA's Nimbus 7 satellite reported a dramatic reduction in the ozone layer over an area somewhat wider than Antarctica. This unexpected "hole" appears to follow an annual cycle showing a minimum ozone concentration in spring (September-October) and, although with some fluctuations and contrary trends, the hole has been progressively increasing in dimension.

By the late '70s ozone variations had demanded the urgent attention of the scientific community and since then every effort has been directed at the understanding of this threat through the adoption of world scale research programs.

Ozone generation and destruction

Ozone is one of the possible molecular combinations of oxygen. It consists of 3 atoms of oxygen (O_3), while the oxygen we normally breathe is biatomic and occurs in the form of O_2. The generation of ozone takes place in the stratosphere, the atmospheric layer between 10 and 50 km above the earth, where the action of sunlight breaks down O_2 molecules into their constituent atoms, which combine again with other O_2 molecules to form ozone molecules ($O_2 + O = O_3$). Conversely, the destruction of ozone is caused by the incidence of UV radiation which hits and breaks down the O_3 molecules, generating new O_2 molecules ($O_3 = O_2 + O$).

This mechanism shows that ozone plays a key role in absorbing most UV radiation and in preventing it from reaching the surface of the earth, where it could seriously damage most biological systems. In this process of shielding the planet from harmful radiation ozone molecules break apart, but are rapidly regenerated by the action of sunlight on O_2 molecules.

Possible causes

Several hypotheses have been put forward to explain the reason for ozone depletion and two basic interpretations have so far been developed. The first tends to explain the phenomenon within a natural frame according to which ozone variations should be related to the global evolution of atmospheric dynamics and to the influence of solar cycles. The second considers ozone depletion to be a result of human activity and, particularly, of the high levels of chlorofluorocarbons (CFCs) released by man into the atmosphere. Although natural causes are not entirely excluded, the the man-made hypothesis has been gaining increasing support in recent years.

CFC hypothesis

CFCs are industrial chemicals composed of chlorine, fluorine and carbon atoms and contained in products of widespread use such as refrigeration units, aerosol sprays and several solvents. One of the principal characteristics of CFCs is their high chemical stability, which allows them to persist in the air and to rise into the stratosphere without being altered en route by chemical reactions or natural agents such as rain.

In the upper layers of the atmosphere, CFC molecules are broken down by UV solar radiation and release active chlorine atoms (Cl) which cause a cycle of chemical reactions resulting in the destruction of ozone molecules. This process appears to be influenced by high atmosphere phenomena, among which the stream of polar air, known as the polar vortex, and the polar stratospheric clouds could play a major role. These high altitude clouds are believed to act as a sort of catalyst in the process of free chlorine generation, particularly during spring when their vaporization is favored by the increase in solar activity. Active chlorine reacts with ozone molecules breaking them down into oxygen (O_2) and chlorine monoxide (ClO), which in its turn reacts again with other ozone molecules furthering the destructive sequence. It is believed that one chlorine atom released by the decomposition of a CFC molecule causes a chain of catalytic reactions by which one atom of chlorine is capable of destroying tens of thousands of ozone molecules. Active chlorine also reacts with other chemicals such as nitrogen oxide (NO_x) and hydrogen (H) and forms relatively inert chlorine reservoirs, which periodically decompose and generate new free chlorine atoms.

Consequences

The magnitude of this phenomenon has called for urgent attention not only to ozone depletion over Antarctica and its still unknown consequences, but also to its impact on net ozone concentration in the atmosphere and global ozone dynamics. Ozone concentration in polar regions differs in many respects from that in equatorial areas, and ozone is usually transferred from higher to lower latitudes. It is still unclear what effects the polar vortex has on ozone variations and what its consequences will be on global atmospheric circulation and world climate.

Preventive measures

Although the ozone issue is still an open question, widespread concern about the harmful effects of CFCs has led several nations to adopt preventive measures, such as the Montreal Protocol aimed at freezing the annual release of CFCs as a first stage in a progressive reduction. One of the major sources of concern is the long life of CFCs, able to persist in the atmosphere for several decades after their release; this means that even if their use were to be completely banned at present, chlorine concentration would continue to increase and react actively for over 100 years.

APPENDIX A

Extracts from recommendations and measures adopted by the Antarctic Treaty Consultative States regarding tourism and the behavior of visitors to Antarctica:

GUIDANCE FOR VISITORS TO THE ANTARCTIC
(extract from Recommendation VIII-9)

The Antarctic and its surrounding islands are one of the few places in the world which are still relatively unchanged by man's activities. Scientists still know very little about the ecological situation in the Antarctic. At the present early stage in research on these matters, some restrictions and precautions may seem unnecessarily harsh, but preliminary studies indicate the need for great caution. By following a few very simple requests, you can help preserve the unique environment of this region.

1. Avoid disturbing wildlife, in particular do not:
   – walk on vegetation;
   – touch or handle birds or seals;
   – startle or chase any bird from its nest;
   – wander indiscriminately through penguin or other bird colonies.

2. Litter of all types must be kept to a minimum. Retain all litter (film wrappers, tissue, food scraps, tins, lotion bottles, etc.) in a bag or pocket to be disposed of on board your ship. Avoid throwing tin cans and other trash off the ship near land.

3. Do not use sporting guns.

4. Do not introduce plants or animals into the Antarctic.

5. Do not collect eggs or fossils.

6. Do not enter any of the Specially Protected Areas and avoid Sites of Special Scientific Interest.

7. In the vicinity of scientific stations avoid interference with scientific work and do not enter unoccupied buildings or refuges except in an emergency.

8. Do not paint names or graffiti on rocks or buildings.

9. Take care of Antarctic historic monuments.

10. When ashore, keep together with your party.

STATEMENT OF ACCEPTED PRINCIPLES AND THE RELEVANT PRO-VISIONS OF THE ANTARCTIC TREATY
(extract from Recommendation VIII-9)

Introduction
The following statement is intended for the guidance of all those who visit the Antarctic.

Recommendations of Antarctic Treaty Consultative Meetings
The Treaty requires that meetings shall be held from time to time to consider and recommend measures in furtherance of its principles and objectives. Amongst these are measures of which all those who enter the Antarctic Treaty Area, both those sponsored by Governments and those not so sponsored, should be aware. The following notes indicate the nature of these measures and the reader is referred to the Recommendations of successive Consultative Meetings for the details.

Protection of the Antarctic Environment
The ecosystem of the Antarctic Treaty Area is particularly vulnerable to human interference and the Antarctic derives much of its importance from its uncontaminated and undisturbed condition and the effects it has on adjacent areas and the global environment. For these reasons the Consultative Parties recognize their special responsibility for the protection of the environment and the wide use of the Treaty Area.

Conservation of Wildlife
Animals in the Antarctic are in almost all cases tame and are therefore peculiarly vulnerable. Both animals and plants are living under extreme conditions and great care has to be taken to avoid upsetting the natural ecological system. They are protected by the following five mechanisms under the Agreed Measures for the Conservation of Antarctic Flora and Fauna:

i) *Protection of Native Fauna*
The killing, wounding, capturing or molesting of any native mammal or native bird is prohibited except in an emergency or in accordance with a permit issued under the authority of a Participating Government. Any attempt to do any of these things is also prohibited under the same conditions.

ii) *Harmful Interference*
Every effort shall be made to minimize harmful interference with the normal living conditions of any native mammal or bird.

iii) *Specially Protected Species*
Two species of seal, Fur Seals and the Ross Seal have been designated as

Specially Protected Species and permits may only be issued in relation to these species in accordance with certain restrictive criteria.

iv) *Specially Protected Areas*

Certain areas of outstanding scientific interest have been designated as Specially Protected Areas in order to preserve their unique natural ecological system. No person may enter such an Area except in accordance with a permit issued under the authority of a Participating Government. Such permits may only be issued in accordance with certain restrictive criteria.

v) *Introduction of Non-Indigenous Species, Parasites and Diseases*

No species of animals or animal not indigenous to the Antarctic Treaty Area may be brought into the Area except in accordance with a permit issued under the authority of a Participating Government. Special precautions have to be taken to prevent the accidental introduction of parasites and diseases into the Treaty Area.

Waste Disposal

In addition to the measures for the conservation of Antarctic Flora and Fauna outlined above, the Consultative Parties have prepared a Code of Conduct for Antarctic Expeditions and Station Activities including, inter alia, recommended procedures for waste disposal.

Protection of Historic Monuments

Every effort should be made to prevent damage or destruction to any historic monuments. The Consultative Parties have listed a number of such monuments for special protection.

Facilitation of Scientific Research: Sites of Special Scientific Interest

There are many scientific investigations being carried out in the Antarctic which could suffer from accidental interference. For example, long term studies of the population dynamics of a penguin colony may require that visitors be kept to an absolute minimum. Intensive scientific work in one area may require that a nearby ecologically similar area be kept undisturbed and uncontaminated for reference purposes. Again, certain electromagnetically "quiet" areas, where sensitive instruments have been installed for recording minute signals associated with upper atmosphere studies, may require that visits to the site should be kept to a minimum. For these and similar reasons the Consultative Parties have designated certain Sites of Special Scientific Interest in the Antarctic. Each Site is subject to a management plan designed to protect the particular scientific investigations being undertaken. Persons wishing to visit Sites of Special Scientific Interest should, well in advance, consult the national office responsible for the administration of a permanent Antarctic scientific expedition or, if this is not possible, should consult the station commander of the scientific station nearest the site which it is intended to visit.

Tourism and Non-Governmental Expeditions to the Antarctic Treaty Area
An important feature of the Antarctic Treaty is that co-operation under it is facilitated by the prior exchange of information about planned activities. The Treaty commitment covers any expedition organized in or proceeding to the Antarctic from any state which is a Contracting Party to the Antarctic Treaty.

Special Measures Relating to Tourist and Non-Governmental Expeditions
The number of non-governmental expeditions to the Antarctic is steadily increasing and there is a tendency for these expeditions to concentrate on the more easily accessible parts of the Antarctic. Frequent visits to scientific stations or undue dependence on the facilities of such stations can prejudice their scientific work. It is therefore required that the organizers of a tourist or non-governmental expedition should furnish notice as soon as possible, through diplomatic channels, to any other Government whose station the expedition plans to visit. Any such Government may refuse to accept a visit to a station which it maintains or may lay down conditions upon which it would grant permission including inter alia, that:

i) reasonable assurance be given of compliance with the provisions of the Antarctic Treaty, measures adopted under it and the conditions applicable at stations to be visited;

ii) tour organizers should ensure that prior to the commencement of the tour or the expedition, procedures and systems for adequate telecommunications have been confirmed with the offices administering the Antarctic stations to be visited;

iii) final arrangements to visit any station be made with that station between twenty-four and seventy-two hours in advance of the expected time of arrival;

iv) all tourist and other visitors comply with any conditions or restrictions on their movements which the station commander may stipulate for their safety or to safeguard scientific programs being undertaken at or near the station;

v) visitors must not enter Specially Protected Areas and must respect designated historic monuments;

vi) tour organizers should report to the Governments whose stations they have visited, after completion of the tour, the name and nationality of the ship, the name of the captain, the itinerary of each separate cruise, the number of tourists accompanying each cruise and the places and dates at which landings were made in the Antarctic Treaty Area, with the number of persons landed on each occasion.

SPECIALLY PROTECTED AREAS (SPAs):

1. Taylor Rookery, Mawson Coast, MacRobertson Land.
2. Rookery Island, Holme Bay, Mawson Coast, MacRobertson Land.
3. Ardery and Odbert Islands, Budd Coast, Wilkes Land.
4. Sabrina Island, Balleny Islands, off Pennel Coast Oates Land.
5. Beaufort Island, Ross Sea, off Scott Coast, Victoria Land.
6. No site (formerly Cape Crozier, now SSSI 1).
7. Cape Hallett, Borchgrevink Coast, Victoria Land.
8. Dion Islands, Marguerite Bay, off Falliers Coast, Graham Land.
9. Green Island, Berthelot Islands, off Graham Coast, Graham Land.
10. No site (formerly Byers Peninsula, now SSSI 6).
11. No site (formerly Cape Shirreff, now SSSI 32).
12. No site (formerly Fildes Peninsula, now SSSI 5).
13. Moe Island, South Orkney Islands.
14. Lynch Island, South Orkney Islands.
15. Southern Powell Island and adjacent islands, South Orkeny Islands.
16. Coppermine Peninsula, Robert Island, South Shetland Islands.
17. Litchfield Island, Arthur Harbour, Palmer Archipelago, off Danco Coast, Graham Land
18. North Coronation Island, South Orkney Islands
19. Lagotellerie Island, Marguerite Bay, off Falliers Coast, Graham Land
20. New College Valley, Caughley Beach, Cape Bird, Ross Island, off Scott Coast, Victoria Land (within SSSI 10)

New proposals for SPAs (at September 1990):

– Lions Rump, King George Island, South Shetland Islands.
– Avian Island, north-west Marguerite Bay, off Falliers Coast, Graham Land.
– Cryptogam Ridge, Mt. Melbourne, Scott Coast, Victoria Land (within SSSI 24)
– Forlidas Pond and adjacent area, Dufek Massif, Pensacola Mountains, Ellsworth Land.

SITES OF SPECIAL SCIENTIFIC INTEREST (SSSIs):

1. Cape Royds, Ross Island, off Scott Coast, Victoria Land (including additional offshore area).
2. Arrival Heights, Hut Peninsula, Ross Island, off Scott Coast, Victoria Land.
3. Barwick Valley, Scott Coast, Victoria Land.
4. Cape Crozier, Ross Island, off Scott Coast, Victoria Land.
5. Fildes Peninsula, King George Island, S. Shetland Islands (two areas).
6. Byers Peninsula, Livingston Island, South Shetland Islands (three areas, but the entire peninsula proposed as SSSI, awaiting approval).
7. Haswell Island, off Queen Mary Coast, Queen Mary Land.
8. Western shore of Admiralty Bay, King George Island, S. Shetland Islands.
9. Rothera Point, Adelaide Island, off Falliers Coast, Palmer Land.
10. Caughley Beach, Cape Bird, Ross Island, off Scott Coast, Victoria Land.
11. Tramway Ridge, Mt. Erebus, Ross Island, off Scott Coast, Victoria Land.
12. Canada Glacier, Lake Fryxell, Taylor Valley, Scott Coast, Victoria Land.
13. Potter Peninsula, King George Island, South Shetland Islands.
14. Harmony Point, Nelson Island, South Shetland Islands.
15. Cierva Point and offshore islands, Danco Coast, Graham Land.
16. North-east Bailey Peninsula, Budd Coast, Wilkes Land.
17. Clark Peninsula, Budd Coast, Wilkes Land.
18. North-west White Island, McMurdo Sound, off Scott Coast, Victoria Land.
19. Linnaeus Terrace, Asgard Range, Scott Coast, Victoria Land.
20. Biscoe Point, Anvers Island, Palmer Archipelago, off Danco Coast, Graham Land.
21. Parts of Deception Island, South Shetland Islands (five areas).
22. Yukidori Valley, Langhhovde, Lutzow-Holm Bay, Crown Prince Olav Coast, Enderby Land.
23. Svarthamaren, Müling Hofmannjella, Crown Princess Martha Coast, Dronning Maud Land.
24. Summit of Mt. Melbourne, Scott Coast, Victoria Land.
25. Marine Plain, Mule Peninsula, Vestfold Hills, Ingrid Christensen Coast, Princess Elizabeth Land.
26. Chile Bay (Discovery Bay), Greenwich Island, South Shetland Islands.
27. Port Foster, Deception Island, South Shetland Islands (two areas).
28. South Bay, Doumer Island, Palmer Archipelago, off Danco Coast, Antarctic Peninsula.
29. Ablation Point-Ganymede Heights, Alexander Island, Palmer Land.
30. Avian Island, north-west Marguerite Bay, off Falliers Coast, Graham Land (redesignated as SPA, awaiting approval).
31. Mt. Flora, Hope Bay, Trinity Peninsula, Graham Land.
32. Cape Shirreff, Livingstone Island, South Shetland Islands (includes Telmo Island and neighboring islets).

New proposals for SSSIs (at September 1990):
– Ardley Island, Maxwell Bay, King George Island, South Shetland Islands.

APPENDIX B

List of the Antarctic National Committees of the SCAR member States:

ARGENTINA   Instituto Antártico Argentino
Cerrito 1248
1010 Buenos Aires

AUSTRALIA   Antarctic Division
Channel Highway
Kingston, Tasmania
Australia, 7050

BELGIUM   Comite National Belge pour les Recherches dans l'Antarctique
Institut Royal des Sciences Natuerelles de Belgique
Rue Vautier 29
1040 Bruxelles

BRAZIL   Commissao Interministerial para os Recursos do Mar
Ministerio da Marinha
40 Andar
70055 Brasilia, DF

CHILE   Instituto Antartico Chileno
Luis Thayer Ojeda 814
Correo Sucursal 21 Santiago

CHINA   Chinese Antarctic Administration
No. 1 Fuxingmenwai Street
Beijing

COLOMBIA   Academia Colombiana de Ciencias
Carrera 3a. A No. 17-34, Piso 3
Apartado 44.763
Bogota 1, D.E.

ECUADOR   Equadorian Antarctic Program
National Scientific Committee on Antarctic Research
P.O. Box 5940
Guayquil

FEDERAL   Alfred Wegener Institute for Polar and Marine Research
REPUBLIC   Columbus Strasse
OF GERMANY Postfach 12 01 61
2850 Bremerhaven

FINLAND   Delegation of the Finnish Academies of Sciences and Letters
Mariankatu 5
00170 Helsinki

FRANCE   T.A.A.F.
34 Rue des Renaudes
75017 Paris

Expeditions Polaires Françaises
47 Ave. du Marechal Fayolle 75116 Paris

GERMAN   Committee on Antarctic Research
DEMOCRATIC Telegrafenberg
REPUBLIC   1561 Postdam

INDIA   Department of Ocean Development
Mahasagar Bhavan
CGO Complex
Lodi Road
New Delhi 110003

ITALY   ENEA Progetto Antartide
C.R.E. Casaccia
P.O. Box 2400
Via Anguillarese 301
00100 Roma A.D.

JAPAN   International Science Division
Science of International Affairs Bureau
Ministry of Education, Science and Culture
3-22 Kasumigaseki
Chiyoda-ku, Tokyo 100

National Institute of Polar Research
9-10 Kaga 1-Chome Itabashi-ku
Tokyo 173

KOREA   Korean National Committee on Antarctic Research
               Korea Ocean Research and Development Institute
               An San
               P.O. Box 29
               Seoul 171-14

NETHERLANDS Netherlands Council of Oceanic Research (NRZ)
               Royal Netherlands Academy of Arts and Sciences
               Postbus 19121
               1000 GC Amsterdam

NEW ZEALAND Antarctic Division
               Department of Scientific and Industrial Research
               P.O. Box 13247
               214A Oxford Terrace
               Christchurch

NORWAY   Norsk Polarinstitut
               Postboks 158
               1330 Oslo Lufthavn

PERU   Comisión Nacional de Asuntos Antarticos (CONAAN)
               Jiron Ucayali 363
               Lima 1

POLAND   Committee on Polar Research
               Polish Academy of Sciences
               Institute of Geological Sciences
               Department of Dynamic Geology
               ul. Senacka 3
               31-002 Krakow

SOUTH AFRICA Department of Environmental Affairs
               Private Bag X447
               Pretoria 0001

SPAIN   Consejo Superior de Investigaciones Científicas
               Serrano 117
               28006 Madrid

SWEDEN   Polar Research Secretariat
               Royal Swedish Academy of Science
               Box 50005
               10405 Stockholm

SWITZERLAND   Commission for Polar Research
Swiss Academy of Sciences
Hirschengraben 11
Postfach 2535
3001 Bern

UNITED   British Antarctic Survey
KINGDOM   High Cross
Madingley Road
Cambridge CB3 OET

U.S.S.R.   The Arctic and Antarctic Research Institute
38 Bering Street
Leningrad, 199 226

URUGUAY   Instituto Antártico Uruguayo
Buenos Aires 350
Montevideo

U.S.A.   Division of Polar Programs
National Science Foundation
1800 G. Street, NW
Washington, DC 20550

APPENDIX **C**

Visiting Antarctica: some practical suggestions

Appropriate behavior for visitors to Antarctica is a very broad concept covering many aspects, both theoretical and practical. First, visitors should be aware of the general principles adopted by the Antarctic Treaty system applying to the Antarctic region and, in particular, their own recommended general behavior.

There are, however, other practical aspects which may appear of minor importance, but which may also contribute to a clearer understanding of the Antarctic style of life. Appropriate Antarctic conduct includes, for example, such apparently self-evident points as knowing what to wear, how to move and where to walk in order not to become a burden to others and to obtain the respect of the Antarctic community.

The first basic consideration of any visitor to Antarctica is equipment. Warm and resistant clothing should be taken as a protection against low temperatures and particularly the wind, which frequently increases the chill factor. Certain basic items of equipment are essential: sunglasses, a warm hat, a scarf and a pair of gloves; a protective belt around the waist can be very useful for people particularly sensitive to low temperatures.

At the same time, excessive layers of clothing which could hamper movement should be avoided, not for aesthetic reasons, but in order to prevent unnecessary risks. There are many restrictions involved in moving on and off transport, and visitors are often asked to move in unfavorable conditions, and on unstable or slippery surfaces. In general it is advisable to avoid running or hurrying, and to move with great caution at all times.

A small shoulder-bag or back-pack can be useful to keep possessions together, and perhaps to carry an extra layer of clothing, candies or chocolate (a good source of energy especially in the cold), and a small bag in which to collect litter such as film wrappers or cigarette ends.

For those interested in photography or filming, a long-distance zoom can be used to observe animal life without approaching too closely; binoculars are also useful in this respect. A threat to animals does not consist only of direct physical damage; for example, birds approached too closely may abandon their nests, leaving eggs or chicks unprotected and subject to the attack of predators.

In general, a zoom lens allows the close observation of any detail of the Antarctic landscape at a distance, without the need to walk or climb in potentially dangerous places, much more numerous than often supposed. This is why visitors are asked not to stray from their party when on land and to follow the instructions of guides or station staff. Antarctica has many hidden dangers; ice moves continuously, crevasses are extremely common, no path is sure, and along the coast overhanging outcrops of ice which appear as firm as rock may collapse at any time. Visitors should bear in mind that any actions carried out on their own initiative involve not only a risk to themselves, but also to those ultimately responsible for rescue operations. Further, unforeseeable circumstances such as an emergency or a sudden change in weather conditions may oblige a party to leave an area with little or no notice, and time taken to search for a visitor subjects the whole group to an unnecessary risk.

Certain general rules should be observed when visiting Antarctic stations. Remembering that in Antarctica there is no human life-sustaining resource but water, any station, even the smallest or simplest, is the result of a tremendous effort which deserves total respect and co-operation for its maintenance. In any station a visitor is above all a guest, and his appreciation may be shown by his considerate behavior, in particular respecting personnel requirements and leaving the station in good order.

In case of uncertainties, consulting a guide or the staff of a station may help a visitor to be clear about appropriate behavior, and thus to become part of the Antarctic community. In this way he will be able to enjoy a more meaningful visit, and to show that "clean" tourism not only implies picking up litter, but also acting responsibly and with the total respect Antarctica deserves.

Glossary and abbreviations

ablation: in a glacier, the loss of volume due to melting, calving or evaporation; opposite: accumulation.

accumulation: in a glacier, the gain of volume as a result of the transformation of snow into ice; opposite: ablation.

Adherent Party or State: referring to the Antarctic Treaty, a Party or State which has joined the agreement, but with no decision-making status; opposite: Consultative State.

albedo: the relationship between received and reflected radiation.

algae: plants which grow in water or moist ground, and have a very simple structure with no true stems, roots, or leaves.

amphibians: the group of cold-blooded vertebrates which live on land but breed in water, such as newts, frogs or toads.

annelida: invertebrates with a segmented body.

arachnids: the group of eight-legged insect-like animals, such as spiders, scorpions or mites.

A.S.I.Z.: Antarctic Sea Ice Zone project.

astenosphere: the layer of semifluid substance beneath the earth's crust on which continental or oceanic plates move.

aurora australis: a luminous phenomenon of electromagnetic origin occurring in the upper atmosphere.

baleen plates: or whalebone formations, fringed horny plates hanging from the palate of the baleen or whalebone whales.

biomass: living stock of a certain species.

B.I.O.M.A.S.S.: Biological Investigation On Marine Antarctic Systems and Stocks.

bryophyts: the group of plants including mosses and liverworts.

calving: the breaking away of an ice block from a glacier to form an iceberg.

catabatic wind: an extremely strong surface wind which blows on the Antarctic coast and may exceed 200 km/h.

catalyst: in chemistry, a substance which aids or speeds up a chemical reaction without itself undergoing any permanent chemical change.

C.C.A.M.L.R.: Convention on the Conservation of Antarctic Marine Living Resources (1971).

C.C.A.S.: Convention for the Conservation of Antarctic Seals (1980).

cetaceans: the order of aquatic mammals including whales, dolphins and porpoises.

C.F.C.: chlorofluorocarbon.

coelenterata: the group of invertebrates having a sac-like body with a single opening, such as jellyfish, sea anemones, or corals.

Consultative Party or State: referring to the Antarctic Treaty, a Party or State which has obtained a decisional status; opposite: Adherent Party or State.

continental shelf: the extension of a continental plate into the sea, up to the continental slope.

C.R.A.M.R.A.: Convention on the Regulation of Antarctic Mineral Resouce Activities (1978).

crèche: a group of young penguins not guarded by their parents, having a protective function.

customary law: the practices which by long-established usage have come to have the force of law.

deglaciated: ice-free.

echinoderms: invertebrate marine organisms with a five-part symmetrical body, such as starfish or sea urchins.

Exclusive Economic Zone (E.E.Z.): the sea zone of 200 nautical miles from the coast over which a coastal State has the exclusive right of exploiting the resources contained in its water column and the soil and subsoil underneath.

ecosystem: a natural system involving the interaction between a living community and its non-living environment.

endemism: a form of life specially suited to living in a determined area.

F.A.O.: Food and Agriculture Organization.

fast ice: the part of the pack ice which remains fixed to the coast.

F.I.B.E.X.: First International B.I.O.M.A.S.S. Experiment.

folding: in geology, the phenomenon by which horizontal and stratified rocks are bent and deformed due to movements within the earth's crust.

food chain: a series of organisms in a community, each member of which feeds on another in the chain and is in turn eaten.

fungi: plants without leaves, flowers or roots which reproduce on spores, including moulds, yeasts and mushrooms.

G.A.R.P.: Global Atmosphere Research Program.

geomagnetism: the branch of physics concerned with the earth's magnetism.

geophysics: the study of the physical phenomena occurring on the earth's surface, in its atmosphere and in its interior.

Gondwanaland: the ancient continent which included Antarctica, South America, Africa, Madagascar, India and Australia (about 250 million years ago).

granite: a very hard igneous rock consisting of quartz and feldspars.

gyre: rotation.

haemoglobin: a protein in red blood cells which carries oxygen from the lungs to the tissues.

halos: optical phenomena which create the illusion of three suns or moons on the same line.

high seas: the part of the sea situated beyond the Exclusive Economic Zone, legally subject to the Convention on the High Seas (1958).

I.A.G.P.: International Antarctic Glaciology Project.

ice floe: a plate of marine ice of variable size, floating in the sea.

I.C.S.U.: International Council of Scientific Unions.

I.G.Y.: International Geophysical Year (1957-58)

intrusion: in geology, the forcing of molten rock into spaces in the overlaying strata.

I.O.C.: Intergovernmental Oceanographic Commission.

ion: an electrically charged atom or group of atoms formed by the loss or gain of one or more electrons.

ionization: the breaking down of a compound into ions caused by a solvent, electrical charge or radiation.

isostatic: in geology, referring to the state of equilibrium of the lithospheric plates on their sublayer.

I.W.C.: International Whaling Commission.

larva: the first and immature stage of a living organism which develops into a different adult form by metamorphosis.

Lautentia: the ancient continent including North America and Eurasia (about 250 million years ago).

lichen: a small plant formed by the association of a fungus and an alga.

lithosphere: the most external layer of the earth's crust subdivided in continental and oceanic plates.

liverwort: a plant growing in wet places and resembling seaweed or leafy mosses.

magma: the hot molten rock within the earth's crust which may find its way to the surface where it solidifies as igneous rock.

metamorphic rock: a rock which has altered considerably from its original structure and composition by pressure and heat.

morphology: the form and structure of living organisms or non-living substances or objects.

nunatak: an ice-free mountain peak emerging from the ice sheet.

orogenic: in geology, referring to the geological processes which lead to the formation of mountain systems.

otarids: the family of sea lions and fur seals, belonging to the order of pinnipeds.

paleoclimatology: the study of past climatic evolution.

Pangea: the ancient continental mass in which all continents were joined (about 300 million years ago).

phocids: the family of seals, belonging to the order of pinnipeds.

photosynthesis: in plants, the synthesis of organic compounds from carbon dioxide and water, using light energy absorbed by chlorophyll.

phytoplankton: plant plankton.

pinnipeds: the order of marine mammals including otarids (sea lions and fur seals), phocids (true seals) and odobaenids (walrus).

plankton: the community of microscopic and mostly unicellular free-floating marine organisms.

plate: in geology, the different parts (continental or oceanic) in which the earth's crust, or lithosphere is divided.

plateau: a wide level area at certain height.

plutonic rock: a rock formed by a molten substance which has cooled and solidified below the earth's surface.

polynia: an ice-free area in a pack ice field.

population dynamics: the global development pattern of a determined population.

protozoa: microscopic organisms formed by a single cell.

rookery: colony.

sastrugis: an accumulation of iced snow eroded by the wind, appearing as a serrated mountain.

S.C.A.R.: Scientific Committee on Antarctic Research.

S.C.O.R.: Scientific Committee on Oceanic Research.

sedimentary rock: a rock which has formed through the accumulation of marine or terrestrial debris deposited in a basin by water, wind or ice, with no major alterations to its original structure and composition.

seismology: the branch of geology concerned with the study of earthquakes.

S.I.B.E.X.: Second International B.I.O.M.A.S.S. Experiment.

S.P.A.: Specially Protected Area.

specialization: in biology, a special physiological adaptation, or a special skill or behavior suited to the environment in which a determined animal lives.

spiracle: the blowhole through which cetaceans breathe.

S.P.S.: Specially Protected Species.

S.S.S.I.: Site of Special Scientific Interst.

subantarctic area: the circumpolar area located at the limit of the Antarctic Convergence forming a separate unit from Antarctica due to different environmental and climatic conditions.

subduction: in geology, the movement of two plates towards each other, by which one is pushed underneath the other.

subglacial: referring to relief existing beneath an ice mass.

subpolar: the area in which environmental features are influenced by the geographical adjacency to the Arctic or Antarctic area.

tectonic: in geology, referring to the forces which produce dynamic changes in the earth's crust.

territorial sea: the sea zone of 12 nautical miles from the coast over which a coastal State may exert sovereign rights.

tortue: a close formation of penguins to maintain body heat and stand winter blizzards.

transform fault: in geology, the movement of two plates in opposite directions on the same plane leading to tectonic instability.

trophic chain: food chain.

Unknown Southern Land: in the 16th century, the general definition of the land situated south of the Magellan Strait.

UV radiation: or ultraviolet, an invisible radiation in the light spectrum.

W.M.O.: World Meteorologial Organization.

zooplankton: animal plankton.

Acknowledgements

I would like to thank the institutions and people whose support and advice has been fundamental to the writing of this book.

I would like to express my gratitude particularly to the staff of the Progetto Antartide of the Italian institute E.N.E.A., which placed its documentation centre at my disposal; to the C.A.D.I.C., the Argentine Southern Scientific Research Centre, which provided me with bibliographical and technical support; to the Antarctic British Survey and the Instituto Antártico Argentino for the helpful information with which they provided me; to In.Tres for use of its computer facilities; to Quid Informatica and C.I.T.E. for their computer advice for the final formatting of the text; to S.C.A.E. for its welcome practical assistance; to Julio Lovece for his kindness in allowing me access to his private library; to Dr. Cristina Delitala, researcher at the Department of Earth Science, University of Rome, for her valuable advice on geological matters; to Dr. Roberto Pistorelli for his legal advice; to Jon Cooper for his invaluable remarks as my first general reader; to my publishers who have shown remarkable patience in listening to all my requirements; and most of all to Maddy Starr who corrected and edited the text and without whose help this book could never have been published.

Last but not least, I would like to thank my friends and family, who have supported and borne with me during all my months of work.

Bibliography

Anaya, H. "Los Pingüinos. Sorprendentes habitantes de los hielos", in *Revista de geografía universal*, Año 2, Vol. 2, Ed. Cono Sur, 3A Editores Méjico, Febrero 1978.

Antártida, No. 16, Dirección Nacional del Antártico, Buenos Aires, Agosto 1988.

Ardito, S. "Oggi un paradiso, diventera una miniera ?", in *Airone*, Anno X, No. 111, Editoriale Giorgio Mondadori, Luglio 1990.

Ardito, S. "Piccolo, grande krill", in *Airone,* Anno X, No. 111, Editoriale Giorgio Mondadori, Luglio 1990.

Atlas enciclopédico Antártico Argentino, Dirección Nacional del Antártico, 3a ed., 1984.

Bellisio, N.B. "Flora y fauna marítima", in *Historia Marítima Argentina*, Tomo I, Cuántica Editora S.A., Buenos Aires, 1982.

Braun Menendez, A. *Pequeña Historia Antártica*, Editorial Francisco de Aguirre S.A., Santiago, 1974.

Caminos, R. "Antártida Argentina", in *Geología Nacional Argentina*, Academia Nacional de Ciencias, Ed. Leanza, Argentina, 1972.

Capdevila, R. and Comerci S.M. *Historia Antártica Argentina*, Dirección Nacional del Antártico, Buenos Aires.

Casellas, A. *Antártida, un malabarismo político,* Instituto de Publicaciones Navales, Buenos Aires, 1981.

Clark, R. *Aves de Tierra del Fuego y Cabo de Hornos. Guía de campo*, L.O.L.A., Buenos Aires, 1986.

Da Cruz, H. *Guía de los grandes cetáceos y actividad ballenera*, Ediciones Miraguano, Madrid.

De Azar, R. *Pingüinos, focas y ballenas del cuadrante antártico americano*, Editorial Albatros, Buenos Aires, 1976.
"Descubrimiento de la Antártida", in *Antártida*, No. 15, Dirección Nacional del Antártico, Buenos Aires, Junio 1988.

Desio, A. *L'Antartide*, UTET, Torino, 1984.

Embleton, C. and King, C.A.M. *Glacial geomorphology*, Halsted Press Book, Y.Wiley and Sons, N.Y.

E.N.E.A. *Destinazione: Terra Nova*, Programma Nazionale di Ricerche in Antartide, Progetto Antartide, E.N.E.A., 1989.

Fraga, J.A. *Introducción a la Geopolítica Antártica*, Dirección Nacional del Antártico, Buenos Aires, 1983.

Greig, D.W. *International law*, 2nd edition, Butterworths, London, 1976.

Handbook of the Antarctic Treaty System, Part 2, Expeditions and Visits, 6th edition, April 1989.

Harrison, P. *Seabirds. An identification guide*, Houghton Miffin Company, Boston Revised Edition, 1985.

Headland, R.K. *Chronological list of Antarctic expeditions and related historical events*, Cambridge University Press.

Hodgson, B. "Antarctica. A land of isolation no more", in *National Geographic*, Vol. 177, No. 4, National Geographic Society, April 1990.

Kimball, L.A. "Special report on: The Antarctic Mineral Convention", International Institute for Environment and Development-North America, N.W., Washington D.C., July 1988.

Leyva, E. "Pingüinos", in *Geomundo*, Vol. 2, No. 2, Editorial Sudamericana S.A., Febrero 1978.

Lichter, A. and Hooper, A. *Guía para el reconocimiento de cetáceos en el mar Argentino*, Fundación Vida Silvestre, Argentina, 1984.

Manzoni, M. *Prospettiva Antartide. Una lettura di geografia antropica*, Edizioni Unicopli, Milano, 1989.

May, J. *Antartide. Il vero volto del settimo continente*, I libri di Greenpeace, Editoriale Giorgio Mondadori, Collana Airone, 1988.

Morosini, M. "Esempio Antartide", in *Scienza e Tecnica*, Annuario della EST, estratti 1987/88.

Mouzo, F.H. "Geología marítima y fluvial", in *Historia Marítima Argentina*, op. cit.

Müller, F.W. "Los antárticos", in *Antártida*, No. 15, Dirección Nacional del Antártico, Buenos Aires, Junio 1988.

Oceanus. The international magazine of marine science and policy, Vol. 31, No. 2, Paul R. Ryan Editor, Published by Woods Hole Oceanographic Institution, Summer 1988.

O.G.S. *Campagna Antartica "OGS-EXPLORA" 1988/89*, Osservatorio Geofisico Sperimentale, Programma Nazionale di Ricerche in Antartide, Rapporto No. 1, Hobart, 1988 (unpublished).

Palazzi, R.O. *Antártida y archipiélagos subantárticos. Factores para su análisis. Los factores estables*, Editorial Pleamar, Buenos Aires, 1987.

Palazzi, R.O. *Antártida y archipiélagos subantárticos. Factores para su análisis. Los factores variables*, Editorial Pleamar, Buenos Aires, 1988.

Pierrou, E. "Antártida", in *Historia Marítima Argentina*, op. cit.

"Pingüinos", in *Antártida*, No. 15, Dirección Nacional del Antártico, Buenos Aires, Junio 1988.

Price, R.J. *Glacial and fluvioglacial landforms*, Clayton Ed. Longman.

Rabassa, J. "Glaciología Antártica", in *Historia Marítima Argentina*, op. cit.

Simpson, G.G. *Penguins. Past and Present, Here and There*, Yale University Press, New Haven and London, 1976.

Zubillaga, J. "Climatología de la Antártida y los mares adyacentes", in *Historia Marítima Argentina*, op. cit.

The drawings in the text were made by the author and based on the bibliographical references mentioned above.

THE FIRST ADVENTURE HANDBOOK OF SOUTHERN SOUTH AMERICA
Emilio Urruty

It describes quite all the circuits you can dare to explore in that remote part of the globe. From the Andes to the Pampas and from Iguazu Falls to Antarctica. Our handbook brings you key advice for virtually every aspect of traveling through an unspoiled virgin land.You will get from the author hundreds of tips to choose the suitable trip for you, notwithstanding your means: from the hardest trek to the most luxurious cruise to Antarctica. Emilio Urruty is an experienced travel journalist. By raft, horse, bike, truck or icebreaker he has traveled from Iquitos to Antarctica crossing the Amazonas, the Andes and Patagonia.
ISBN 1-87956805-5 — 352 pages — 4 1/2" x 7 1/4" — Hardcover 4 col. — Index — TOC — Illustrations — Maps — $ 34.95

TIERRA DEL FUEGO
Lago Argentino - Fitz Roy - Perito Moreno Glacier - El Paine - South Chile

Nobody programmes his visit to Tierra del Fuego with the sole purpose of visiting the island. It is quite common to plan a trip around the South of Argentina and Chile. That is why our travel Guide does not limit its information solely to Tierra del Fuego. It includes interesting data on other spectacular attractions which one can plan to see when traveling to or from the island.
ISBN 1-879568-03-9 — 128 pages — 8" x 5 1/2" — Full color illustrations and photos — Geographical index — Maps — Map of Tierra del Fuego 24" x 28" — (English/Spanish/German) — $ 20.00

TIERRA DEL FUEGO MAGAZINE

Tierra del Fuego Magazine is not just another travel publication, it is destination specific, aimed to the European and American traveler. It features articles by local travel writers and wonderful full color photography of Southern Patagonia, Tierra del Fuego and Antarctica. Appears once a year.
ISSN 0327-344X — 80 pages — 8" x 11" — Full color illustrations and photos — Maps — (English/Spanish) — $ 8.00 (Available vol. 1 and 2)

If you want to know the best way to order our publications or any other book or map about the South of South America, write or call us.

Quantity discounts available for booksellers and special customers.

ZAGIER & URRUTY
P U B L I C A T I O N S

6630 Indian Creek Dr. # 223 – Miami Beach, FL 33141-5840 – Phone/FAX (305) 865-5002

Outside the United States: P. O. Box 94 Suc. 19 – 1419 Buenos Aires – Argentina
Phone (54-1) 572-1050 – FAX (54-1) 572-5766